MILLICENT ZAHN BOOK OF PLASTICS CRAFT

Color Pages

Dedicated to:

MY LOVING HUSBAND, LEONARD,
who said that I could do it,

MY MOTHER,
who said that I could do it "better,"

and

ROBERT GEORGE FLEISCHER,
who suggested that I do it in the first place.

MILLICENT ZAHN
BOOK OF PLASTICS CRAFT

Millicent Zahn

Edited by
Sterling McIlhany

VNR VAN NOSTRAND REINHOLD COMPANY
NEW YORK CINCINNATI TORONTO LONDON MELBOURNE

Van Nostrand Reinhold Company Regional Offices:
New York Cincinnati Chicago Millbrae Dallas

Van Nostrand Reinhold Company International Offices:
London Toronto Melbourne

Copyright © 1973 by Litton Educational Publishing, Inc.

Library of Congress Catalog Card Number 72-9711
ISBN 0-442-29582-0 (paper)
ISBN 0-442-29583-9 (cloth)

Designed by Visuality

Photographs by Fortune Monte

Published by Van Nostrand Reinhold Company
450 West 33rd Street, New York, N.Y. 10001

16 15 14 13 12 11 10 9 8 7 6 5 4 3 2 1

CONTENTS

My thanks to:

JAMES GRAD,
who introduced me to this rewarding career.

ANTON MILCETIC and BOB STICHLER,
who helped me with the products shown in
this book and who have taught me much
about the fabricating and producing of my
designs.

ED YARK, DAN YORK, and GARY FISHER.

And special thanks to
JOHN R. GILL
of the Rohm and Haas company for his
invaluable technical assistance.

This book is addressed to the enthusiastic
craftsman who, though creative, is totally
unfamiliar with working with acrylics. Owning
no equipment, one can purchase the
material, either in large sheets or prepared
(cut and polished to order), and proceed at
once. After experiencing the swift, happy
success of his first piece of work, he may
become bolder, may buy some tools and start
to work from scratch.

Introduction

Every period in the complex history of Western society has inherited, perhaps created, an art medium that keenly expresses its unique character. For the classical civilizations of Greece and Rome, long-lasting, warm-hued marble was the ideal medium to capture the spirit of man and his gods. For the Byzantine world that followed, the brilliant art of mosaic reveals in the splendor of rich color and sparkling light the world of courtly life and a new-born religion. Stained glass *is* the Middle Ages, a profound result of man's spiritual vision and the reflected light of the sun. In the 15th century, during the Renaissance, the still popular oil painting medium was invented, which provided the ideal means for depicting in fine detail the new image of man and nature. The next three centuries saw the full development of dramatic emotion in art by the large-scale fresco and sculpture in a variety of fine media. The 19th century experienced a return to past styles and media in a calculated effort to regain the spirit of earlier periods.

The 20th century has seen a change in the function and media of art. In the spirit of past ages, we have created a new medium that perfectly expresses the nature of our time. What is the new medium? Plastic. Everyone comes into personal contact with plastics each hour of the day, from tooth brushes, combs, and shavers to clothing fabrics, dinnerware, radios, clocks, luggage and furniture, as well as decorative and functional parts of cars and commercial jet liners. We are an Age of Plastic.

In recent years serious artists have turned to acrylic plastic as an ideal medium for three-dimensional fine art. Not only is plastic already familiar to everyone, but it has intrinsic qualities that are very attractive to the artist in search of a new medium. It is readily obtainable, easy and fast to work with, opaque or transparent, and light in weight. Acrylic plastic lends itself easily to combination with other media, such as acrylic paints and a variety of surface insets. In all, working with plastic can increase the imagination and working skills of the beginner and create new vision for the experienced artist.

Millicent Zahn is an outstanding example of the latter, an artist already experienced in traditional painting and three-dimensional media, who began to explore the new world of plastics, thus increasing her skills as a fine artist and broadening her vision of art in life.

All of Millicent Zahn's projects are arranged in sequence in this book. Beginning with basic tools and techniques, they gradually increase in technical and aesthetic complexity. The projects present a clearly defined course in acrylic plastics for the learner, whether beginning or experienced. In a similar sequence are the illustrations of Millicent's acrylic sculpture, which begin with her first work in the plastic medium and conclude with the latest at the time of this book's publication. Their progress in technique, size, and design illustrate the artistic progress that anyone can look forward to by following the learning skills clearly outlined.

Millicent Zahn began using acrylic plastic for sculpture near the end of 1968. Early work used scraps of plastic to create a free-hanging mobile of a circle with triangle inserts. These two basic shapes are placed in creative symmetry that produces a kinetic feeling—a combination of form changing, motion, and textural variety. The artist then began to take a course in plastic art from a local teacher and picked up additional working skills under the guidance of local plastic engineers. She realized at that time that her personal medium was plastic rather than the previous one, metal.

Since that time she has worked independently for herself and under a number of commissions, creating a wide variety of pieces from large-scale sculpture to fine single pieces. The artist does most of her creative thinking spontaneously, frequently while driving, then puts her new ideas to work in her home studio.

Following early experiments with plastic, Millicent Zahn decided to enter the commercial field "because I got greedy!" The first commercial product was an adult puzzle made up of rectangular pieces that, when properly assembled, formed a large rectangle. Among those who sold it was the Museum of Modern Art. Millicent was inspired by the puzzle to push on to other works: an ice bucket, coasters, lap tray, and holder for eyeglasses. In order to deliver the new works to stores that sold them, and being a new member of the fast-paced business world who knew little of the techniques of commercial delivery, she hired a driver. Personnel guarding the rear delivery doors of Fifth Avenue stores were pop-eyed with surprise at Millicent Zahn when she arrived and emerged from the car laden with bundles to be delivered via the back door.

In summary, Millicent Zahn describes her encounter with plastics: "As an artist looking for an ideal medium, I worked first in clay, then direct plaster. The resultant solid sculpture did not appeal to me aesthetically, so I next tried welded metal. It made me realize that I was a constructivist by nature, and so finally I began to create with plastic.

"Acrylic sheet has some of the properties of metal. It is rigid and precise. Its sharp angles are its greatest qualities; angles combined with transparency produce a beautiful effect. Combined with light refraction, angles and transparency produce a clean, pure medium that goes well in nature and man-made surroundings. I like it because it's an instant success. The purity of the material seems to dictate what should be done with it, and whatever is done with it seems to work."

Sterling McIlhany
New York, 1973

PART 1. WHERE TO GO, WHAT TO BUY, WHAT TO DO

1. Materials and Tools, Their Functions

Why sheet acrylic? Because of its qualities of shiny transparency when used clear, its depth of color when opaque, its light refraction making light and line another dimension of your work, its magnifying quality when curved. Why? Because of its ease of fabrication, its versatility. Because it was today thirty years ago. It is today now.

Purchasing your material. Acrylic sheets can be found in most hardware, lumber, and glass stores, as well as some art supply stores, and hobby stores. Also look for plastic supply houses in the Yellow Pages listed under "plastics; rods, tubes and sheets."

Walking into a store selling acrylic materials has the dazzling effect of entering a "penny candy store." You don't know what to look at first because aside from the sheets of acrylic, transparent or opaque, smooth or textured, colorless or in a rainbow of colors, one can buy findings: those bits and pieces of cubes and balls, rods and reeds. After the first excited look around, a good plan is to buy some material with which to practice the techniques that are described later: cutting or scribing, sanding and polishing, bending and heat forming, bonding.

Sheet acrylic is called by various trade names. It may be referred to as Plexiglas, the material manufactured by Rohm and Haas, Lucite, the name popularized by Dupont, Perspex, made abroad by I.C.I., Acrylite, by American Cyanamid, and other brands as well. Because I usually ask for Plexiglas, in this book I will refer to sheet acrylic material by that name.

Since the sheets come in thicknesses ranging in standard stock from $\frac{1}{32}$ inch to four inches and in the types mentioned above, you can see the possibilities presented to you. The sheets are large, usually 4 × 6 feet or 4 × 8 feet, but most suppliers sell them in half sheets or will (for an extra charge) cut them smaller. But begin with some $\frac{1}{8}$-inch and $\frac{1}{4}$-inch transparent sheets with which to practice. In most plastic supply stores scraps are available, sometimes sold by the pound. It is a good idea to avail yourself of scraps for more than one reason. Beside the obvious reason, that of economy, the various sizes and shapes will "talk" to you and give you ideas for future work. Besides purchasing the scraps, buy some

jewel-like balls, and any other findings such as cast cubes, rods, etc. Buy a length of tubing, which comes in various diameters and thicknesses of wall, and buy any other fancy shapes that might catch your eye. When buying the balls or half-balls, be sure to find out whether they are made of acrylic or of polyester resin. Each has a different requirement for cementing. This will be discussed in the section on bonding.

Don't leave the plastics supply store without ordering some pre-cut pieces with which to make a small cube as a "first." When figuring your measurements, be sure that you take the thickness of wall into consideration. For example, if your material is $\frac{1}{4}$ inch thick, and you wish to make a 3-inch cube, you will need two pieces measuring 3 inches squared for the top and bottom, but for the other pieces, subtracting for the thickness of the wall, the sizes needed are two 2½ × 2½ and two measuring 3 × 2½ inches.

When purchasing material for craft use, be careful not to purchase the sheet acrylic intended for glazing purposes only, as its chemical resistance making it ideal for use in glazing will not permit it to be welded by the solvents you will be using for fabricating. The material intended to be used for crafts is "G"; the glazing material is "K."

There is a new material coated for abrasive resistance for use in table tops. It is called Abcite and is considerably more expensive than the usual material, approximately a dollar per foot more.

For bonding (or cementing), the chemicals EDC (ethylene dichloride) or MDC (methylene chloride) are used. MDC is said to be less flammable, faster drying, and less toxic than EDC. Blended solvents are sold under various brand names and are available in the small bottles suitable for the home craftsman. These blended solvents contain a combination of MDC and other chemicals and usually a small amount of acrylic monomer. Two of the brand names are IPS Weld On #3 and Rez-n'Bond. There are others. Your plastics dealer will carry at least one brand. A thickened form of solvent will also be needed. The uses for both forms of solvent will be described more fully under Bonding. Also needed will be a thin brush, eye-dropper or squeeze bottle with needle-like applicator

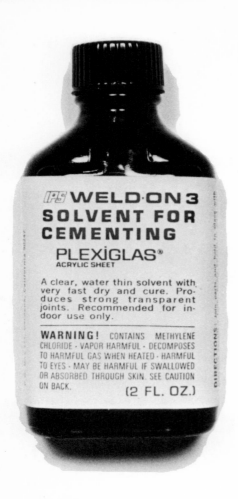

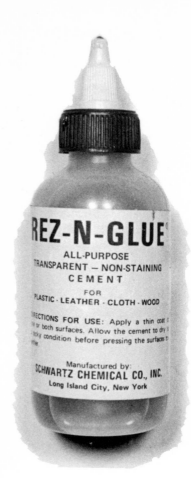

1 One brand of solvent for cementing sheet acrylic.

2 Thickened cement.

3 and 4 Two scribes for cutting thin material.

5 Anti-stat cleaner.

5

6 Strip heater.

which has been designed for use with the thin solvents. The latter may be purchased wherever plastics are sold.

For cutting thin (up to ¼-inch) grades of acrylic sheet, a tool called a scribe may be used. The scribe is available in prices varying from $1.75 to $9.00. The principle in the use of all grades is the same. My preference is for the middle grade, simply because I find that in that model the handle is the most comfortable for me. A visit to your hardware store will allow you to judge for yourself.

An anti-stat cleaner is available from plastics dealers. You will find this invaluable, as one of the less desirable characteristics of this medium is its tendency to draw through static electricity any dust particles in the air.

For those living in areas where these purchases may be difficult, see Sources of Supply in the back of the book.

Later purchases will include a strip heater, electric saw, and electric drill with buffing attachment.

The strip heater will provide you with a step in the fabrication of your Plexiglas, making it possible to make bends in the material. It is one of the more important additions to your studio. The strip-heating element manufactured by the Briscoe Manufacturing Company is sold by plastics dealers. It is packaged complete with instructions for its easy assembling. The materials needed

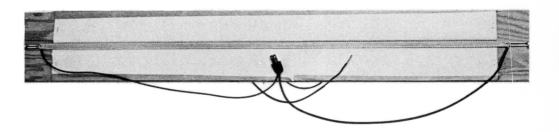

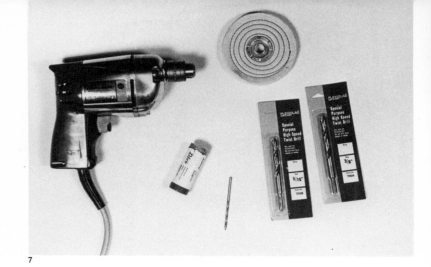

7 Electric drill with drill bits and buffing attachment with polishing compound.

8 Vise.

9 Hand saw.

include some plywood, asbestos paper, and aluminum foil. You can make the strip heater yourself or have it made by a carpenter or handyman.

An electric drill with variable speeds from 0 to 2250rpm may be purchased. It is most important to have a variable-speed drill because although when used for polishing your material with the buffing attachment fast speed is required, drilling of holes must be done at a slower speed. Even if you purchase the new drill bits recently made for use with acrylic sheet that permit faster drilling, you will have to slow down your speed when drilling holes ⅜ inch or larger. More thorough information regarding drilling will be contained in the section on drilling. Be sure to purchase a vise to attach to your work table. The drill can be clamped into the vise in a horizontal position and in effect becomes a stationary buffer (with proper attachments added) for polishing. Your pieces may then be held firmly in both hands while being polished.

An electric saw will give you more spontaneity. If you have advanced to the point where you own an electric saw, you can, instead of having to plan in advance, decide on a project and begin at once. The first saw to buy is the reciprocating jig saw, sometimes called a "sabre" saw. The blades should have at least 14 teeth per inch. When more experienced, and if room in your workshop permits, you might purchase a bench or table saw. Be sure to purchase blades recommended for plastics. Teeth should be the same shape and height, and there should be at least six teeth per inch. Purchase some tallow, or beeswax, for coating the blade. This will reduce friction, cut down on chipping and overheating. If you have trouble finding the beeswax, small cakes of it may be purchased from a shop selling sewing supplies. It is the same beeswax used by sewers to coat their thread.

A tool for the removal of the protective masking paper from just part of your acrylic sheet is manufactured by Fletcher-Terry. It is adapted from the glass cutter and is worked under the same principle. Kerosene or mineral spirits will be needed for use with this tool. More instructions for its use will be contained in the section on bending.

8

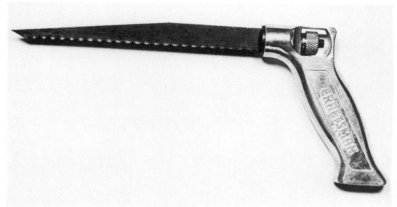

9

10

12

10 Sabre saw and reciprocating saw.

11 Bench or table saw.

12 Beeswax or tallow to lubricate blade.

13 Tool for removing masking paper.

14 Kerosene for removal of masking paper cement.

13

11

14

2. Start Experimenting

When you have returned home with your purchases, you will want to experiment at once. Do you have a small art object that should be on its own base? Your pre-cut pieces will make a small cube upon which to stand it.

Use the thin solvent for cementing.

Easy, isn't it?

But—

Is it leaning a little to one side? Did you have a little something left over when you were putting the last piece in place?

If you had used a right-angle aid when cementing your pieces, it would have a more precise look. And in order to prevent your pieces not all joining together properly, it would have been a good idea to use tape to hold the cube together before cementing. In that way you could have shifted a little where necessary if the pieces did not fit with precision. It is also important to know that the best way to make a cube is to make a frame first out of all the pieces that go around the sides, and then to add the top and bottom to the frame. That will also permit you to adjust for any irregularities.

But, you do have a cube that you made yourself. And that is only the beginning.

15 Make the "frame" first after taping pieces together for proper alignment.

16 Top and bottom are then cemented in place.

15

16

3. Techniques for Fabricating

17 On plastic protected by masking paper, a scribe and metal ruler are used to make several strokes along the line where the break will take place.

Preparation for Cutting. Acrylic sheet is always sold with protective masking paper on both surfaces. Leave this on as long as possible. The paper may be marked with pen or pencil as a guide before cutting. If, however, you have for some reason removed the paper and wish to cut or drill your material, be sure to re-protect with masking tape or with mystic paper, which may be purchased in widths up to 30 inches. Failure to protect the material before cutting with an electric saw will result in the cut heat-welding itself from the friction of the saw blade, and failure to protect before using an electric drill will result in cracking or fracturing.

Cutting with Scribe. If the material is thin (up to ¼ inch), it may be cut with the scribing tool. Using a ruler or other straight edge as a guide, make several strokes along the determined line. You will probably need five or six strokes to score ⅛-inch material sufficiently before breaking, and as many as ten for ¼-inch. After scoring, place the material, scored side up, over a dowel which is, if possible, the length of the incised line. If this is not possible, be sure to move the dowel along with your hands following the progression of the break as you press firmly down, hands parallel. The piece is now ready for scraping, sanding, polishing, etc. This technique cannot be used on textured material.

Sawing. When cutting with a sabre saw, hold your material firmly and apply saw with a smooth, even feed. Wood clamps to hold the material to your work table will give you two hands with which to guide the saw. When using a bench saw, be sure that the blade height is just a little above the thickness of the material. Tallow (beeswax) applied to the blade will give smoother operation, avoid chipping and overheating of the blade.

Drilling. Drilling may be done with a hand drill or with an electric drill. If possible, use the new high-speed, special-purpose drill bits that were developed for use with Plexiglas. They are manufactured by Henry L. Hanson Co., Worcester, Mass. If you do not own these new bits, speed must be kept to a minimum to avoid chipping and to avoid having the shavings climb up your drill. The special bits are designed so that

18 A dowel placed under the scored line allows a sharp, clean break to be made.

19 Paper-protected material is cut with sabre saw while clamped firmly to work table.

20 Clamp.

21 Holes may be drilled with the electric drill. The masking paper helps prevent chipping and cracking of the Plexiglas.

they can be used at speeds up to 3000rpm, except when holes are ⅜ inch or larger. In that case speed should be kept down to 1000-2000rpm. Be sure to clamp your material to your work table before drilling, and back it with a piece of soft wood. Do not force feed.

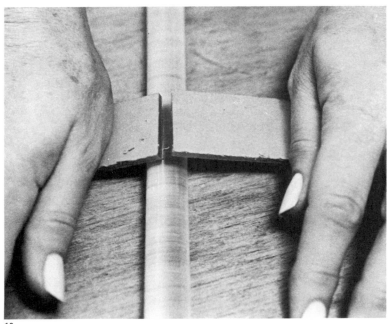

18

19

20

21

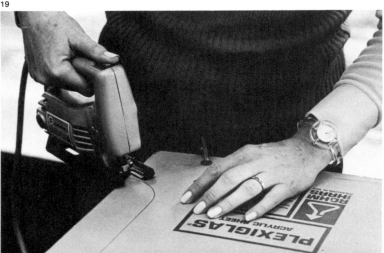

22 To make interior cut, a hole is drilled to allow the saw blade to enter. The saw then finds its way to the perimeter of the hole, and the sawing proceeds.

23 Material is held firmly in vise while the edge is being scraped. This will remove marks left by the saw blade.

The drill is also used as a preliminary to cutting an internal hole. To cut an internal hole, mark a line indicating where the saw cut will be. With your drill, bore a hole inside the area which will be large enough for saw blade to enter. Do not bore your hole on cutting line, but inside the area to be cut out. Then insert your sabre saw in the drilled hole and cut outward toward pencil line. You may then follow guide line to make your cut out.

Edge Finishing. As the blade of the saw sometimes leaves marks on the edge of the material which polishing will emphasize, it is important to scrape the edge of Plexiglas before polishing. This is done easily with a wood scraper or with a discarded hacksaw blade which you may prepare for this purpose. In order to do this, file the back side of the blade to sharpen. Ignore the tooth side; this will not be used. The two ends of the blade should be wrapped with tape, as this will produce two places, one on each end, where you will hold the blade while scraping. Place your material in a vise before scraping, then scrape with a gentle, constant pressure. It is important that you do not achieve a curve while scraping, as you will then be unable to make a proper contact when bonding. Your material is now ready to polish to a fine gleam.

After scraping has produced a uniform, smooth edge, sanding is the next operation. At this point you might give some thought to the lovely matte or semi-opaque finish that careful sanding provides. The use of silicone carbide "no-load" paper #220A and a consistently smooth and caressing stroke resulted in the matte edges on all of the triangular pieces which are part of *Mobile #1*, pictured on page 38.

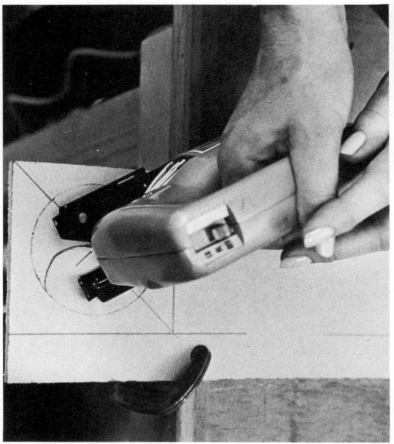

22

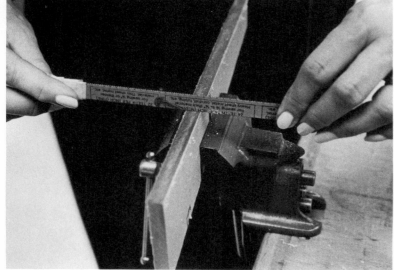

23

24 Scraper made from
hacksaw blade.

25 Three grades of
sandpaper.

26 The edge is then sanded
with silicone carbide paper
which has been folded
around a block.

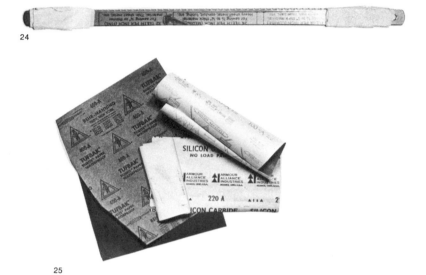

24

25

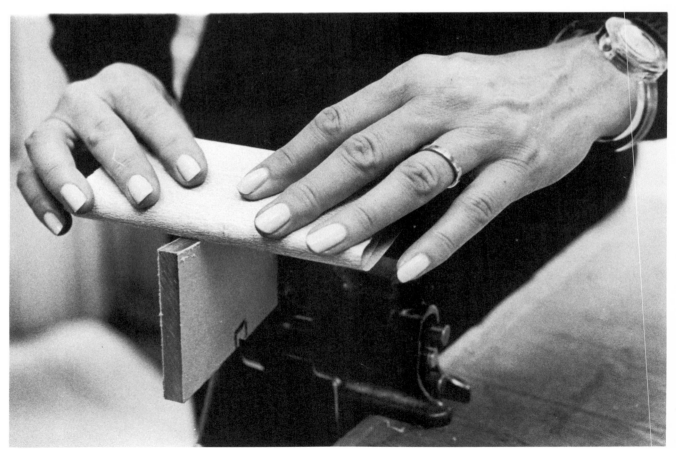

26

27 The edge is now ready to be polished to a fine gleam using compound on the buffing attachment of the electric drill.

Polishing. For a highly polished edge, it is necessary to sand with a finer paper than the one just mentioned. The #220A should be followed by "wet and dry" 400 and progress to 600. Using it dry rather than wet makes it easier to notice the progress of the operation. The edge is now ready to be highly polished. If you have not yet purchased a drill with buffing attachment, you can polish the edges by hand, using jeweler's rouge. This may be purchased in a small jar under the trade name Lustrar. Be sure to apply it to the polishing cloth and not directly to your material. Hand polishing is very time consuming, however, and you would do well to make an electric drill an early purchase. With the buffing attachment prepared and packaged under the brand name Dico, a small amount of buffing compound is included. However, you may purchase buffing compounds separately wherever hardware is sold. It is the same compound used to polish brass, silver, and other metals. Buffing compound comes in various grits or grades of abrasiveness. These grades are determined by color, and the use of color to designate them is universal. The grade known as "tripoli" or "reddish brown" is the best to use with your buffing wheel. If an even higher gloss is desired you may

28

28 Isopropyl alcohol for removal of grease pencil marks on plexiglas.

progress to white. However, do not use the deep red or the black with an electric buffer. Sometimes you may have to buy the compound in a package containing bars of all colors. Reserve the latter two colors for other uses.

Buff at high speed, and keep your piece moving while it is being buffed to avoid overheating. Be sure to apply compound to the buffing wheel and not to the edge of your material. Your drill should be clamped in a vise if the article to be buffed is small enough to be held in your hands, and the piece to be polished should be held firmly, as the high speed might throw it out of your grasp. As a final step in polishing, a clean wheel may be attached. Incidentally, if you have trouble finding buffing compound, you might try using toothpaste or silver polish available at your supermarket. It is not necessary to polish to transparency edges which will be cemented. Scraping and sanding will leave an ideal surface to bond.

I cannot stress too firmly that safety precautions must be observed with the drill as with all power equipment. Your eyes should be protected by goggles from flying particles and dust, and care should be taken to prevent loose clothing or long hair from becoming tangled in the drill.

Flaming is another method of polishing. While this is not always satisfactory, causing crazing in some cases and discoloration in others, it is a fast way of polishing an edge, and if used with caution may have satisfactory results. Always prepare properly before flaming, as saw marks will be very apparent when flamed. A propane torch is used for this operation; Bernzomatic is one brand. The torch should be held at least six inches from the material, be kept in motion to prevent overheating and bubbling, be used with fire-prevention precautions kept always in mind and in a well-ventilated area. The protective paper should be torn away from the edge to be flamed, and wetting of any paper on the plastic sheet will help avoid accidental burning. This type of polishing should never be attempted by the beginning craftsman and should not be done unless your work area is absolutely safe. It should be noted that chemicals should certainly be nowhere near this area.

Repairing Damage. Minor surface scratches may be removed with some success. A kit called "polysand" containing various grades of abrasive cloth is available for this purpose. You also might try using a mild abrasive such as toothpaste followed by an application of paste wax. Avoid waxes containing silicone, as this might cause crazing (fracturing of the material).

Cleaning. Do not dry dust acrylic. Just as with the lacquer surface of an automobile where dry dusting will cause tiny cross hatches on the surface, your Plexiglas articles would soon dull with scratches resulting from their surfaces having been scratched by the particles of dust ground into the surface from dry dusting. Cleaning with an anti-stat cleaner will not only clean your work, but will help the material to combat its natural tendency to draw dust by electrostatic action. Isopropyl alcohol, available in drug stores, may also be used to clean Plexiglas, and a popular commercial product sold in stores under the brand name Pledge is very successful for cleaning and protecting this material.

Sometimes the protective masking paper is very resistant to its removal and may leave a residue of dried cement on the surface. This will happen if you do not observe the precaution of keeping your stored material away from temperature extremes. If this should happen, it might be necessary to use a solvent such as kerosene or steam-distilled turpentine to help loosen the paper. After the solvent is applied, start to strip and roll the paper off. It might be necessary in stubborn cases to apply the solvent along the line where the paper is separating from the sheet. Remove the solvent from the sheet as soon as possible by wiping the surface with isopropyl alcohol followed by soap and water, and rinse with clear water. Be sure to work, while doing this, in a well-ventilated room.

Bonding

There is something magic in the "instant fusing" when solvent is applied to two adjoining pieces of sheet acrylic. In this chapter you will learn the fundamentals of fusing and something about the hazards as well as the ease of this operation.

29

29 Thinned solvent may be applied with thin brush . . .

30 or eyedropper . . .

31 or, best of all, the needle-like applicator.

32 The solvent finds its way along the seam.

When bonding two pieces of similar material, acrylic to acrylic, the thinner form of EDC or MDC is used. It is applied with thin brush, eye-dropper or, best of all, the squeeze bottle with needle-like tip made for this purpose. Wherever the thin solvent is applied to the joint, it travels by capillary action along the surface where the two edges meet. When the solvent touches the two surfaces, it literally breaks down the material, and the two surfaces fuse together as one. Care must be taken to avoid spills, as even one drop of solvent will mar the crystal-like surface of the material. It is advisable to have a damp cloth handy. Pat the spot immediately or not at all. If action has begun, it is dangerous to touch. Another pitfall to avoid if possible is the entrapment of air in a joint. It is almost impossible to avoid altogether, and on humid days more air bubbles form than on dry. One precaution to take when using the squeeze bottle is to squirt a little liquid out of the applicator before beginning, much as a doctor does before giving an injection. It is also a good idea to squirt a little fluid out of the applicator after cementing to clean the needle of a chance bit of plastic dust which may have been accidentally drawn into it. This would eventually clog the needle, making it unfit for use.

Try to have a uniformity of solvent along the joint. You will have to touch more than once long areas to be cemented, but soon after your first experiment with this technique, you will be able to judge how much solvent to apply, how far it travels, and how long it takes to fuse. "How long" literally means seconds because this is a swift technique. The piece sets up in seconds, is dry in minutes, and firm enough to machine in four hours.

When applying solvent by this method, it is best to do so when the material is in a horizontal position. If, for example, you are making a cube, keep turning the piece after the joint sets up so that you will avoid the hazard of having the solvent run down along a vertical seam. Apply the solvent starting near, but not at, the end of the seam joint, and watch it crawl in both directions. If you are holding the material with one hand while working with the other, hold it firmly, but not so firm as to squeeze any of the solvent out of the joint.

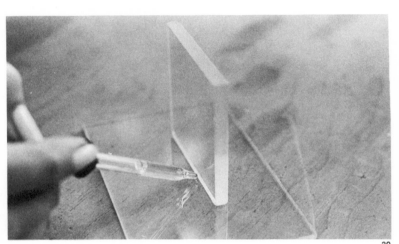

30

31

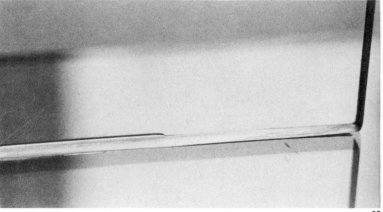

32

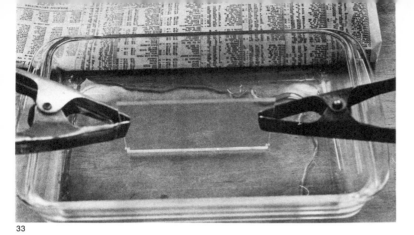

33

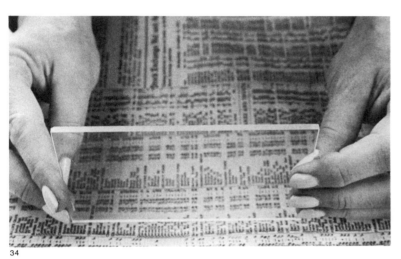

34

33 The Plexiglas, while being supported by clamps, is soaked until it softens.

34 It is quickly blotted to prevent droplets from damaging the material . . .

35 And it is held together until it welds.

35

Experience will show you just how much pressure will insure a firm enough fit to allow a consistency of liquid into the joint. The transparency of the material will let you watch the progress and tell you when to touch it again to complete the length of the seam. After a while this will become instinctive, and when you begin to work on opaque materials, you will automatically be able to perform this technique. The moment you have started, fusing has begun. And by the time, seconds later, you have lifted your needle, or eye-dropper, the fusion is complete. The chemical softens the acrylic and makes the two as one. A few minutes later, when the material has resumed its rigidity (time varies with weather conditions, longer when humid, and varies with thickness of material), you can turn it over and do a second joint. Although the piece may be firm enough to continue to cement all around, you must allow four hours for it to be sufficiently permanent if more machining must be done. It should be noted here that solvent should not be put back into the original bottle after a day's use. It is more economical to empty the applicator, discard the unused solvent, and flush the applicator out with water than to chance contaminating your supply of solvent.

Another method of bonding with the thinner solvent is soak cementing. This is done by soaking the edge to be cemented in some solvent until it softens, and then with light pressure holding it in place until fusing occurs. This gives a very strong joint. For this procedure you will need a pan large enough in which to stand the piece of material, and clamps with which to hold it upright in a shallow amount of solvent. The soak method of cementing, while important when cementing areas which may be hard to reach with the needle-tip applicator, is rather messy, and much care must be taken when carrying the just-soaked piece over that material on which it will be placed in order that drops of solvent do not ruin your work. It is also advisable to have some kind of a jig prepared to hold your pieces together while they are setting so that the soaked piece does not slip out of place.

36 Thickened solvent is used to cement acrylic to materials of dissimilar nature.

37 Inexperience and poor planning add up to a messy result.

Bonding Dissimilar Materials

If you wish to cement together two dissimilar materials, such as acrylic to polyester, or to cement other materials to acrylic, such as shells, glass, etc., the thicker type of solvent, which contains a percentage of acrylic monomer, is used. This type of solvent is also used for cementing acrylic to acrylic when a very strong joint strength is required. It is slower drying than the thinner solvent. However, because it is slower drying, it may be used when the piece to be bonded cannot be reached by the needle-type applicator, but must have the cement applied first and then put into place. If you were to do this with the thin, faster drying cement, it would be dry before you were able to make the contact necessary for bonding. This type of cement is applied with a rod, spatula or brush. If a brush is used, clean immediately with EDC. Those familiar with the epoxy cements will wonder why they are not used when cementing foreign materials to Plexiglas. Actually, you might use them if working with opaque material, but with the clear the slightly yellow tint of the epoxies will show.

At this point you should be cautioned that when working with transparent material, you should not attempt to bond together anything on which the surface to be cemented is too wide. You will find that with anything wider than ¼ inch, air bubbles inevitably entrapped in the joint are very apparent. Some planning is required when designing, and two large surfaces might well be planned with a small strip at the point of contact. In opaque materials, of course, there is no problem, but with transparent, ingenuity is required to avoid this problem.

A case in point is *Reeds*. The original construction was the second piece I had ever made, and when planning it I did not consider that the smoke panel could not be cemented to one of the clear sides successfully. By the time I had the parts before me and had started to work, it was too late because I had had the pieces cut to my order, did not own any tools, and had not the experience to know how to handle the situation that arose when I started to assemble the construction. I tried in vain to put a minute amount of solvent on each of the four corners of the smoke panel. But

remember, it crawls! The result was a poorly crafted piece, and with this experience behind I planned the subsequent *Reeds*.

Attaching the smoke-colored panel proved to be more satisfactory once I decided to have grooves cut into the base. Grooves meant that the piece had more stability, as the cement had more surface that it could cover (the sides and bottom of the groove). I ordered the grooves cut where my material was purchased. However, if this had not been possible, I could have improvised by cementing two strips with a channel between. I have since learned that grooves may be cut using a bench saw, in which case the blade is lowered so that just the amount of blade needed for the depth of the required groove is exposed.

The effect achieved was that of more depth, as the upright pieces gave another dimension to my construction. The rest of the piece was worked out as before with the flexible rod placed at random lengths into the holes drilled to hold them in place on the top piece. When planning the second *Reeds*, I also decided to use ¼-inch material instead of ⅛-inch as before. I had the edges highly polished. The resulting difference is evident in the two photographs.

Assuring Proper Fit. Since right angles are a must if things are to hold together with precise fit, it is a good idea to have some aid in assuring a proper right angle. A right-angle aid was made for me out of

38 This is the second *Reeds*, executed with precision (Collection of Mr. and Mrs. William L. Safire, Washington, D.C.).

39 A piece of thin material is inserted between the angle aid and the piece to be cemented. This prevents accidental damaging of material by solvent flooding.

40 Altered miter box used to aid in assuring a proper right angle.

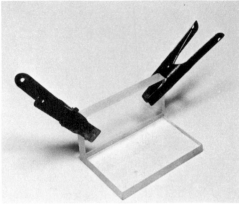

39

40

38

½-inch scraps by a technician when I started working in plastics. He presented it to me with many verbal instructions and admonitions regarding care and neatness.

When using this, a ⅛-inch piece of material should be clamped between it and the upright piece being cemented. This piece should not go to the bottom where the cementing takes place. Its purpose is to prevent actual contact between the angle aid and the piece to be cemented, as a chance drop of solvent leaking out the back of the joint would smudge the surface of your material.

It is also possible to make out of plywood, or improvise with an altered miter box (purchased at a lumber yard), a right-angle wall to be used for the same purpose as outlined above. A slight bevel at the bottom will act in the same manner as the extra ⅛-inch piece mentioned above, that of keeping the bottom edge of the Plexiglas from contact with the wall.

Right-angle clamps into which the sheets of acrylic may be placed for cementing may also be purchased if the above system proves inadequate for your purposes.

41 Clamping the softened material to the right angle assures a proper bend.

42 The masking paper may be removed from just the section of the material to be heated. Be sure to do this on both sides.

43 Before heating takes place, the marks made by the china marking pencil must be removed.

44 China marking or grease pencil.

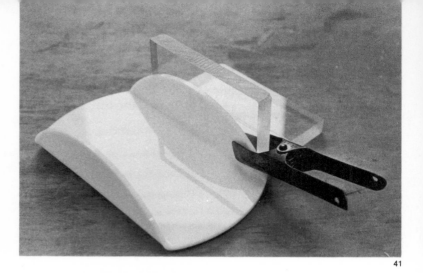
41

Bending and Heat Forming

The purchase of the components for making a strip heater gives the craftsman a larger area of working possibilities. As described in Chapter 1, this is easy to make. The principle behind using the strip heater is that acrylic softens for bending at a temperature of 290°-340° F., is easily bent at that stage, and quickly hardens back to its rigid form. It is necessary to hold it in place while it cools, which takes but minutes, and you can do this with clamps or even with your hands.

Experiment with your strip heater in order to acquaint yourself with this technique. Your material should be edge finished before proceeding, and the protective paper should be removed from both sides of the acrylic along the line to be heated. To peel a strip of paper (from both sides) along the space to be strip heated, the Fletcher-Terry masking tool may be used. Scribe lightly in a 2-inch strip, wet with kerosene, and peel. Place the piece on the pre-heated heater after having marked the spot to be bent. If you use china marking pencil, wipe it off before the heating actually takes place. The time needed for your material to obtain the degree of softness necessary for bending varies with the thickness of the material: a ⅛-inch-thick piece will take as little as five or six minutes, a ¼-inch piece 12-15 minutes. Bend the piece, the heated side out, to the required angle, and hold in place until cool. Since acrylic has a "memory," mistakes are able to be corrected by re-heating, in which case the material slowly resumes its flat form and can be re-bent.

42

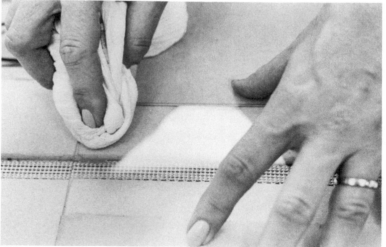
43

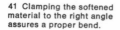
44

45 Quickly bend piece,
heated side out.

46 Hold in place until cold.

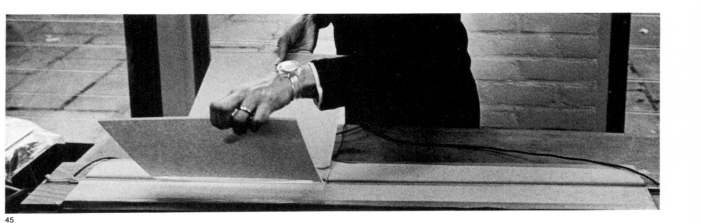

45

46

47 Heating to forming temperature makes it look like rubber.

48 You can cool it quickly by immersing in water.

47

Heat Forming

Acrylic softens to forming stages after being submitted to heat of approximately 300° F. Before placing material in the oven for heating, the protective paper must be peeled off, and all edge finishing done prior to forming. If you are fortunate enough to have a kitchen oven which contains a window and which can be lit from within, this project will be much easier, as you will be able to watch its progress.

A Teflon-coated cookie sheet on which to lay your piece will protect it from scratches. Your hands should be protected by wearing cotton gloves. And I cannot stress too strongly the need for safety precautions. Never, for a moment, leave your work unattended. It is also advised that after pre-heating the oven and after your piece to be softened has been inserted, you wedge a small bit of asbestos potholder between the oven door and the top of the frame in order to permit any accumulated gases to escape.

Experiment to see how long it takes for heating. The proper consistency makes the material look like rubber.

When cooling, your work should be held in place either with clamps or other aids until it becomes firm. You may, if necessary, cool your work quickly by immersing it in lukewarm water, as acrylic can take sudden temperature changes.

To experiment with this technique, try to heat some rod. When purchasing rod, I suggest that you use cast rather than extruded rod. Although more expensive, cast rod is more uniform in appearance; having less visual distortion, it machines better, cements better, and shows less stress when heated. Cut your rod (¼-inch diameter) to a ten-inch length. Place it in a 300° F. pre-heated oven. If you are able to watch it through a door window in your oven, you will be able to see noticeable changes in the material after about four minutes. Don't be afraid to open the door and test its consistency. If it just has some "give," it is not quite ready. Try it again in a few minutes. A ¼-inch rod should become the consistency of "limp spaghetti" in about six

48

CAUTION: Great care should be taken in heating acrylic to its forming temperature. Plexiglas should not be exposed to temperatures above 300°F. If an oven or other heating enclosure is used, provide ventilation so gasses can not accumulate. Also provide open ventilation in the room. Do not use a gas oven and do not have an open flame in the work room. If Plexiglas is overheated, gasses may be released which if ignited can cause severe explosions. Have a general purpose ABC rated (dry powder) fire extinguisher nearby.

minutes. If it is ready, quickly remove it from the oven and tie it into a knot. If you have to force it, put it back, as trying to shape acrylic when it is not ready will cause crazing (tiny fractures). It is interesting to see that if you do put it back into the oven, it will resume its straight, original shape. This is because of the "memory" quality of this material. Save this practice piece, as you will be able to use it as a guide when making your first project using this heating technique (Make a Necklace) which will be described later in this book.

49 Quickly remove it from oven and tie it into a knot.

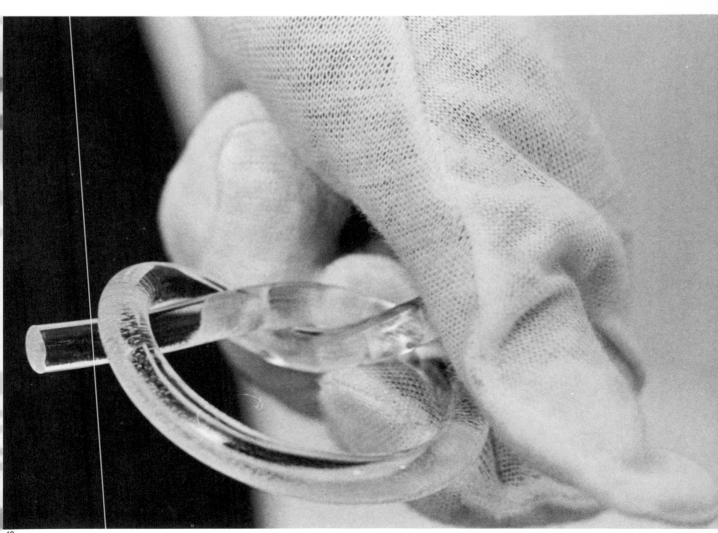

PART 2. YOU CAN DO IT TOO

50 *Construction Deux*
(Collection Mr. and Mrs.
Herman Meckler, Kings Point,
New York and London,
England).

51 Using the scribe and a
metal ruler, the strips are
scored prior to breaking.

52 The piece may then be
broken over a dowel.

4. Construction Ace

Since this is an early project, I have planned
the basic measurements for you; however,
the nature of this construction always allows
you to give it your own signature in placing
the findings and to punctuate it with your
use of color.

It is advisable for you to have some help in
cutting your pieces this early in your
experience with Plexiglas. You may either
have all of the pieces pre-cut following the
specifications outlined, or you may have
strips cut which you will then cut using your
scribe in order that you have the proper
lengths for this construction.

The construction in the accompanying
illustrations uses about 7 feet of ¼-inch
thick clear material, 2 inches in width, and
uses about 3 feet of ⅛-inch-thick material,
4 inches in width. If, however, you have some
experience and own a power saw, purchase
14 square feet of ¼-inch and 12 square feet
of ⅛-inch material. You will also need two
solid 2-inch cubes, which may be purchased
already polished. A large assortment of
findings that includes bits and pieces of rod,
half-balls, etc., will complete your purchases.
Be sure to include some in transparent
color as well as in colorless. At the time of
your purchase, inquire whether the colored
half-balls are made of acrylic or polyester.
If polyester, as the colored balls sometimes
are, the thickened form of cement must be
used for bonding.

You may use your scribe and the method
described in the section about cutting (p. 11)
to cut the ¼-inch strips into pieces with
the following measurements:

two 2 × 14 inches
two 2 × 10¼ inches
one 2 × 7½ inches
one 2 × 11½ inches

Of the ⅛-inch thick material that you have
had cut into 4-inch strips, some will be left
that width, and some will be cut in half.
Proceed to make them into the following:

three 4 × 4 inches
four 4 × 4 inches
four 2 × 2 inches
one   2 × 5½ inches

51

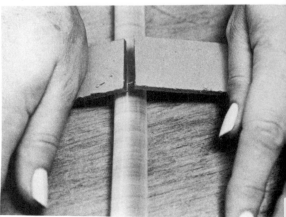

52

31

53 The "frame" is made first, using thin solvent and needle applicator.

54 As some of the findings are made of polyester resin and not acrylic, the thicker form of cement must be used. More drying time is required.

55 A "sandwich" is made which will form one of the decorated sections.

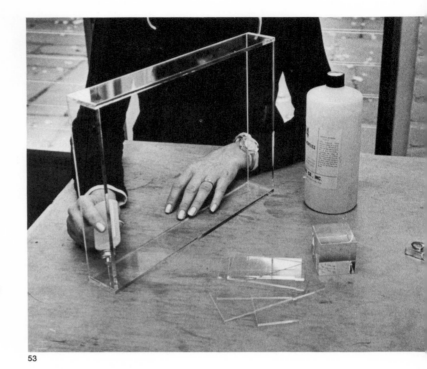

53

After you have all of the components before you, finish the edges. You may either leave them with the matte finish or go on to polish them. But you may not have purchased a drill with buffing attachment as yet, and hand polishing would be rather a chore for all of these pieces. You might, in fact, prefer the satiny gleam of the sanded edge. The choice is personal.

1. With the aid of your needle-like applicator and the thin cement, make the frame first with the two 2 × 14-inch and the two 2 × 10¼-inch pieces. Put aside to set.

2. Cement together the remaining two ¼-inch pieces. The 11½-inch piece should be placed two inches from the end of the 7½-inch piece and be perpendicular to that piece.

3. While the above are setting, you may proceed to the creative part of this project. Following the same procedure for each, you will make "triple-decker sandwiches" of the 4-inch squares, the 2-inch squares, and the 4 × 2-inch rectangles. The procedure to follow when assembling these "sandwiches" is as follows: lay one of the pieces on a dust-free work area, and proceed to cement on some of the findings. As you will need some help in keeping the pieces of acrylic sheet parallel so that when they are cemented in place on the construction they will fit properly, it is a good idea to choose first at least three half-balls of the same size to be placed strategically to hold the squares equidistant from one another. You may then put the rest of the findings in at random, forming the pattern or illusion you find most pleasing. Then attach squares #1 and #2 together by means of a drop of cement on the top of those key half-balls, and proceed as before until you have all three sheets decorated and together. Repeat with the other sizes.

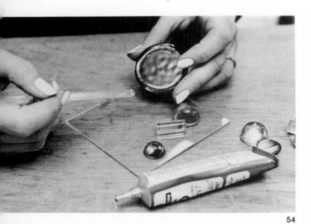

54

55

56

56 The inside partition is
then attached to the frame.

57 Detail may be painted with
acrylic paint and sable brush.

4. By this time, the frame is set and so is
the other section which has formerly been
cemented (see step 2). That section should
be placed inside the frame and cemented
so that there is now a section within the
frame measuring 5¼ × 11½ inches, and an
extension measuring 2 inches where one of
the decorated "sandwiches" will be placed.

5. You will notice by observing the
accompanying photograph that there is an
abstract line running through the pattern of
the 4 × 4-inch section. If you wish to have
one on your piece, this may be painted in
with a fine sable brush and acrylic paint.

57

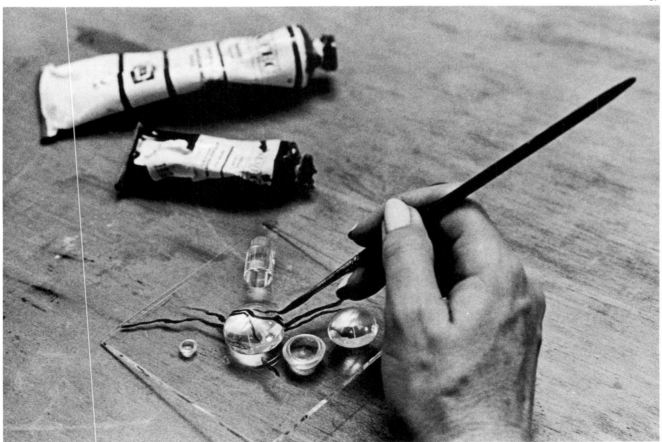

6. Now is the time for you to place your patterned sections. You may follow the design of the one photographed, or place them according to any whim, as this is where creativity takes place. As in the one photographed, you might want to use the large colored polyester balls for spots of color.

Now that you have enjoyed this early endeavor, explore the possibilities of making another standing construction along the same principles. *Juxtapositions,* made of transparent, smoke-colored Plexiglas combined with clear tubing of random lengths, is another example.

58

58 An illusion of underwater fantasy is suggested by detail.

59 Finished piece.

59

60 *Juxtapositions,* another
piece with similar principle,
using varying lengths of
tubing for detail. (Collection
Mr. and Mrs. Mark Lederman,
New York).

61 *Standing Woman* (Private
collection).

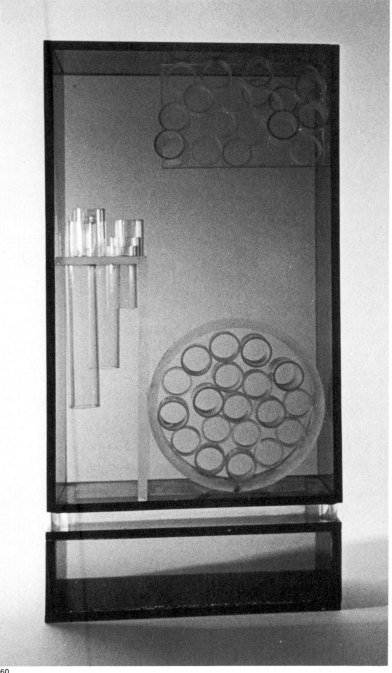

60

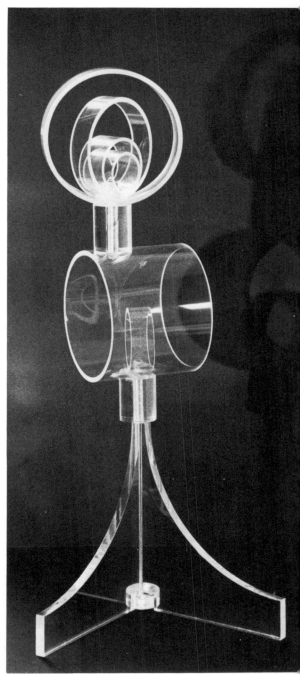

61

5. Make a Mobile

62 *Mobile 1* (Collection of
Mr. and Mrs. Marshall P. Safir,
Kings Point, New York).

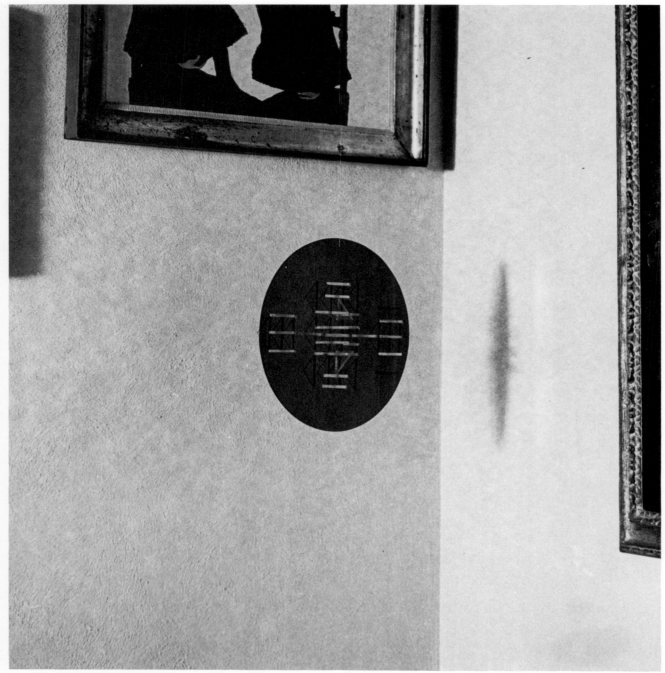

62 *Mobile 1* (Collection of
Mr. and Mrs. Marshall P. Safir,
Kings Point, New York).

62

One day, early in my experience with acrylics, I fell heir to a cache of triangles that were destined for the scrap heap. I later learned that they had been cut from hundreds of squares that had been trimmed prior to being cut into circles. I took them back to my studio, as I knew that the repetition of this classic shape could be well used for the design of a construction. How right I was! The triangles were not only used for several constructions, but were inspirations for large structures when I used those very discarded pieces as small models for larger works.

One of the first pieces that I made using some of my large supply, hoarded until inspiration hit, was *Mobile #1.*

Mobile #1, to be followed by several in that series, is a source of great satisfaction. Although it is of simple design, the constant movement caused by air currents produces fascinating reflections and changing patterns. The transparency of the material adds to the design because the pieces on side A show through to side B, giving another dimension to the simple pattern. The basic approach to creating the mobile is as follows:

63 Material marked for cutting. Circle is indicated by heavy pencil line drawn with the aid of a compass.

1. Cut and polish (or have cut and polished at time of purchase) a circle 16 inches in diameter from a ¼-inch-thick, smoke-colored acrylic sheet. The color I used is Plexiglas gray #2538, or you might use with equal success bronze #2412. The circle will require a small hole drilled into it in order for it to be hung. But it is best not to do this until after the piece is completed. Somewhere along the way you might decide that what you thought was the vertical looks better being the horizontal. And for the triangles that form the pattern, if you are not fortunate enough to fall heir to a treasury of discarded triangles, cut or have cut in clear ¼-inch thick material approximately thirty 2-inch squares, which will then be cut diagonally to form the triangles.

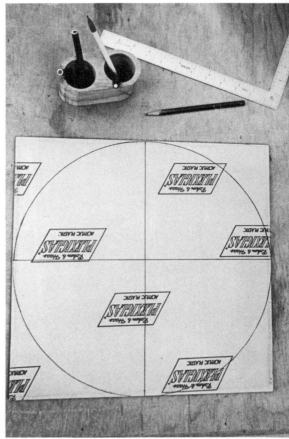

63

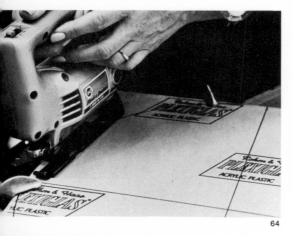

64

64 Paper-protected circle is cut out with sabre saw.

65 Masking paper is removed from Plexiglas circle by rolling it off with a plastic rod.

66 One of the triangles to be used to decorate the mobile is clamped on a vise to have the edges scraped.

67 When scraping is completed, the edges are sanded.

68 Protected papers having been on the triangles too long are resisting removal. Kerosene is required to help this process, after which the triangles are washed with detergent and rinsed well.

65

2. For a satin finish on the edges of the triangles, after scraping to remove any saw marks, sand with 220 no-load silicone carbide paper, and dust carefully. Do not be tempted to polish these edges. The combination of the satin-finished edges with the shiny surface is most desirable.

3. The next step is to remove the masking paper in preparation to attaching the triangles to the circle to form the pattern. Ordinarily this is a simple procedure, but as I had made the mistake of storing my prize stack of triangles in an unheated area of the basement, some of the cement stubbornly adhered to the surface of the material, making the removal of the paper most difficult. I found it necessary, therefore, to engage the aid of kerosene to help clean the material and loosen the resisting masking paper. If you find it necessary to do this at any time, follow the directions for this procedure outlined on page 13, and be sure that you rinse well as suggested. I protected my hands with rubber gloves while using the kerosene. Note: rinse gloves to prevent the kerosene from attacking the rubber.

66

67

68

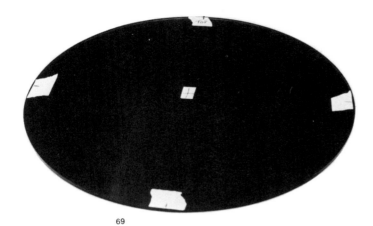

69

4. Using graph paper with heavy lines marking off the 1-inch sections, trace the circle, and mark off in color or dark ink a center cross, and also mark off a few points on the edge of the drawn circle with corresponding marks on your Plexiglas circle so that you will be aware if your work shifts. This marking may be done with china marking pencil. However, since the material is dark in color in the case of this mobile, I made my marks with ink on masking tape that had been placed on the material for this purpose.

5. Begin with side A, and, working with your graph paper under the piece so that you may use the lines and spaces as a guide, begin to place your triangles, using some with the short side down, some with the long side down, but keeping your design symmetrical. This will give balance when the air currents make your finished piece turn. After you have placed them to your satisfaction, you may cement with your thin solvent and needle. Wait for about 20 minutes after cementing before turning the piece over to do the other side. Now you will have to forego using the graph paper. Instead you may use the completed work on side A as a guide. It is easy to do this, since the Plexiglas you are using is transparent, and you can look right through it as you work. In order to support your work without having it rest on the just-cemented pieces, prop it on something elevated, such as the edges of a box, etc. When working out the design on side B, remember that the design is the sum of both sides. Make both count!

69 With small pieces of masking tape placed on the surface of the circle, marks are made designating the top, bottom, and sides. These correspond to similar marks made on the graph paper which is underneath.

70 The triangles are arranged on side A.

71 After turning the circle over, side A, which can be seen through the transparent material, acts as a guide for the placement of the triangles on side B.

72 After placing a small piece of masking paper on the spot to be drilled, the hole is made through which the monofilament will be strung for hanging.

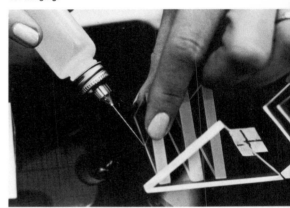

70

71

72

73

74

73 Finished mobile.

74 Another in the series. This is not hung; it rests on a block of clear Plexiglas.

75 This one in the series uses a rectangle in combination with the triangles.

75

6. Happy Anniversary

The occasion of our thirtieth anniversary inspired the lettered cube within a cube, within a cube, ad infinitum. For this project I used ¼-inch material all in clear except two sides of the outside cube which I made in transparent amber, just for an extra punch! The lettering, available in art supply stores, is called "Plas-Stick." It consists of letters imprinted on clear plastic with pressure-sensitive back. The finished cube measures 4 × 4 inches, the inside cubes start with a solid 1¼-inch cube and progress to 2-inch, 3½-inch, and finally to the outside 4-inch cube. Since there is some play between the 1¼-inch and the 2-inch cubes, there is a small amount of movement adding to the kinetic sensation. And for an added dazzle, small findings (tiny cubes and half-balls) are cemented to the outside of the 2-inch cube before it is inserted into the 3½-inch one.

The lettering starts on the smallest cube, the words winding their way around it. And when you letter the second cube, bear in mind that the message is read through both; so the words jump back and forth from layer to layer.

76 Self-adhering letters are attached to the solid inside cube.

76

77 A

77 B

78

77 A and B The second cube is made to enclose the first. The top and bottom sections of the cube are cut slightly large to permit cementing from the outside.

78 The small cube is placed into the second with room to spare, causing slight movement which will add to the kinetic character of the piece.

79 The third cube has larger lettering, making the words on all three bounce back and forth.

Make all of the parts complete before inserting them into one another. In that way you can experiment to see what to add for your final design.

When measuring for your cubes, remember the instructions previously given regarding subtracting the width of the material when figuring. For example, if using ¼-inch material to make a four-inch cube, the measurements are: two (for top and bottom) 4 × 4 inches, two at 4 × 3½ inches, and the other two 3½ × 3½ inches.

Be sure to clean off your cubes before you cement them in or you will immortalize your fingerprints along with your message!

79

80 A parade of cubes.

81 Two of the sides of the
outside cube are made of
transparent amber color. The
sunny appearance it causes
goes well with the word
"love."

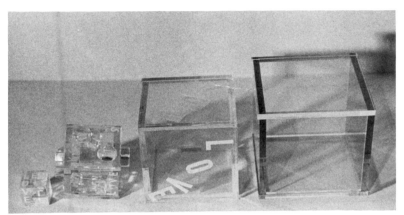

80

81

7. Interpreting Design: the Dibbler

Once you have completed several projects made of Plexiglas, you will find that you have begun to look at many things with an eye toward interpreting them using this medium. Most things translate very well. The most important thing to remember is that a crisp, clean line is best. No embellishments can do other than detract from your design.

An example of an old favorite made into a "Tiffany" version was suggested by Peter Dibble. The "dibbler" is a holder for a standard roll of adding machine paper, used as a memo pad. This is but one version of this familiar item. Perhaps you can think of other variations of the "dibbler."

82 The dibbler, ready for use.

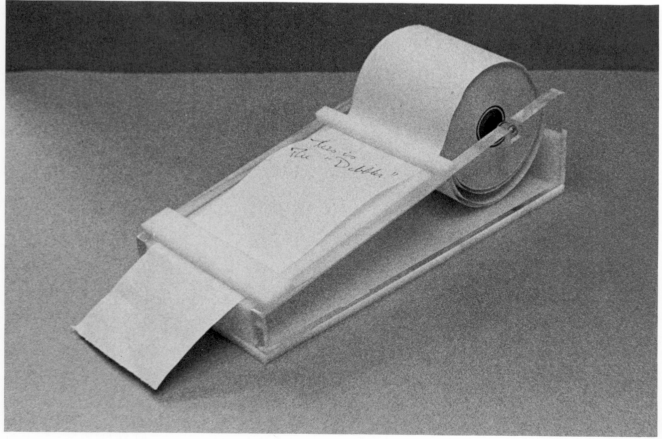

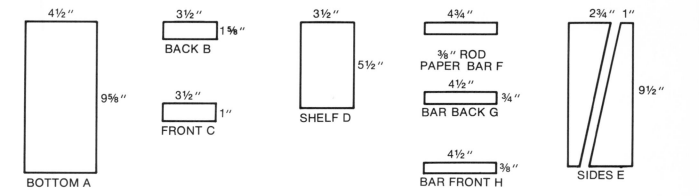

4½"
9⅝"

BOTTOM A

3½"
1⅝"

BACK B

3½"
1"

FRONT C

3½"
5½"

SHELF D

4¾"

⅜" ROD
PAPER BAR F

4½"
¾"

BAR BACK G

4½"
⅜"

BAR FRONT H

2¾" 1"
9½"

SIDES E

All pieces except sides (E) and bar (F) are white, opaque material ¼ inch thick. Sides are clear, ⅜ inch and bar is cast rod, ⅜ inch in diameter. When cutting, note that the sides (E) may be cut from one rectangular piece and then divided and sanded on one end to form curve. See illustration.

1. To insure uniformity of notches that will hold the paper bar, tape together both pieces of sides (E) to mark. The notch should be ½ inch wide and ½ inch deep and be placed ¾ inch from the back (curved) end on the slanted side, which is the top of the piece. After you have marked on the masking paper where the notches will be, you may separate the pieces and proceed to make the notches as shown in the following:

Clamp piece E horizontally to your work bench, and using ⅜-inch drill bit, drill a hole 1¾ inch from back corner on top (slanted) edge, ½ inch from top edge.

Using saw, cut in two lines from top edge to drilled hole. This will cause a small piece of material to fall away, leaving a rough notch measuring about ⅜ × ½ inch.

Turn piece in vise so it becomes vertical, and using coarse and then fine file, smooth edges of notch. This will file away enough material so the notch will now measure ½ inch squared. This need not be polished.

83

83 While one of the sides is held firmly in a vise, the corner is filed to form a slight curve.

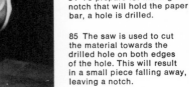

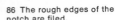

84 To prepare for making the notch that will hold the paper bar, a hole is drilled.

85 The saw is used to cut the material towards the drilled hole on both edges of the hole. This will result in a small piece falling away, leaving a notch.

86 The rough edges of the notch are filed.

87 After all pieces are edge-finished, the first joint is cemented. This is clamped against the Plexiglas right-angle aid to assure a proper fit.

84

85

86

87

2. Using a file, remove enough material to achieve a curve on the back (wide) side of both pieces (E) which will form the sides. Use sandpaper to smooth edge.

3. Edge finish all pieces as described on page 18.

4. Place one of the clear sides (E) against your right-angle aid, and attach back (B). After this has set, turn and repeat with front, and then with other side until frame is complete. Note: be sure to keep in mind that the slanted side of (E) is the top.

5. After frame has set, turn it on its side, and working from the under side place the shelf (D) at the angle formed where the front meets the sides. Place the shelf with the side having the 10 degree angle butting the front piece.

6. The frame may then be cemented to the bottom (A). Note that there is a slight extension of the bottom around the frame. This will enable you to do your cementing from the outside of your piece.

7. G and H are bars to hold the paper flat to the shelf. They are attached directly over the front and back end of the shelf. However, they are not cemented to the shelf, but at each end they are attached to the top edge of sides (E).

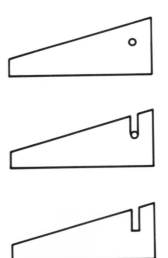

8. Mark off ¼ inch on each end of the rod used to hold the paper roll, and file away enough to form a slight jog. This will allow the paper roll to sit firmly in the notch, the jog preventing the rod from slipping through.

9. Attach a half-ball at each end of rod (F). This rod is slipped through the roll of paper and placed into notches. The paper is then fed under bar (G) at the top and bar (H) at the bottom of the shelf.

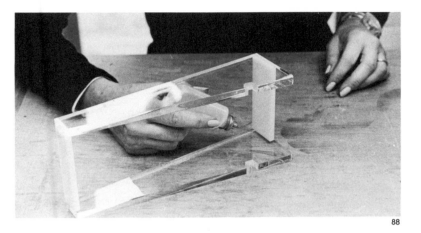

88 Second joint cemented will complete frame.

89 The shelf is adjusted prior to cementing.

90 Bottom is then attached.

91 In order to keep the piece level while the strips are cemented, it is propped up.

92 Small half-balls are attached to the ends of the rod which will slip through the paper roll.

93 The paper is threaded under the two bars.

88

89

90

91

92

93

8. Variations on a Theme

The three different designs for the calendar use simple techniques. Ingenuity will provide many other ways of treating this necessary accessory.

94

95

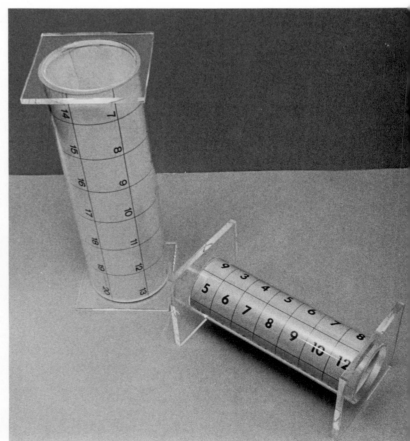

96

97 Before removing masking paper, holes are drilled where screws will be inserted.

98 After edge-finishing the opaque piece that will be the bottom and the clear piece that will be the top bar, half-balls are cemented to the under side of the opaque piece of Plexiglas.

99 All that is left to do is to place the paper, insert the screws,

100 and add the clear piece and the two chrome balls.

97

Desk Diary

Before planning this desk diary, purchase a standard refill from your stationer. Plan your dimensions around the size purchased. The one pictured is #58½ and is made by Ever Ready. It measures 8 × 5 inches.

1. Using ¼-inch royal blue, cut a rectangle 8½ × 5½ inches. This will allow a small border. For the bar holding the pad, ⅜-inch clear is used. Cut this 5 × 1⅝ inches. Drill holes through both after aligning with holes provided on calendar refill.

2. Polish all edges.

3. Small half-balls cemented on the four corners complete the diary.

4. Assemble, using 1-inch chrome-plated balls held on with 1¾-inch screws. These may be purchased from a hardware supply store.

98

99

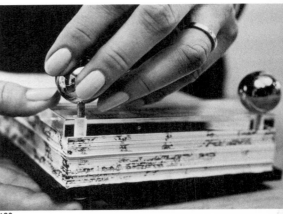
100

101 After the holes have been drilled and the Plexiglas edge-finished, the protective masking paper is removed from one side. On the other side, using kerosene and the special masking paper removal tool, the paper is scored.

102 A strip of paper is removed between the scored lines which is the area to be placed over the strip heater.

101

Wall Calendar with Attached Marking Pencil

This calendar is made to hold a standard calendar containing one month per page. Purchase one with squares designating days large enough for small notations. The calendar pictured measures 10½ × 11 inches.

1. Using ⅛-inch clear material, cut a rectangle 16 × 11 inches. Holes should be drilled on one end for hanging. There should also be a small hole for attaching string that will hold a pencil.

2. On that same end (which will become the top), round off the two corners. This can be done with a sander. Polish all edges.

3. This will be placed on the strip heater for bending. The bend should be 11½ inches from the bottom end. Note that ¼ inch is allowed for bend, and ¼ is allowed for the paper to be held. After removing the protective paper completely from the inside, and in a strip on the outside of the bend in the manner described in the chapter on bending, place the Plexiglas on the strip heater. When material is soft, quickly bend and hold in place with clamps until cool.

China marking pencil is attached by means of monofilament.

102

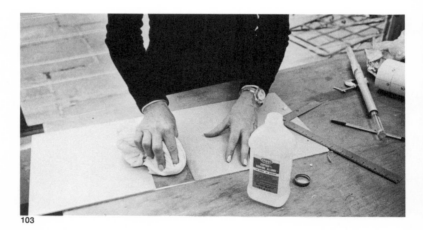

103

103 Isopropyl alcohol followed by water will clean the kerosene from the surface of the material.

104 After designating the spot to be placed over the center of the heating sections by marking with a china marker, the Plexiglas is put into place. Before heating begins to take place, the marks are wiped off.

104

105

105 The piece has softened, and it is ready to be removed from heater.

106 It is quickly bent . . .

107 and held in place with the aid of two spring clamps until it is cool.

108 All of the twelve pages of the calendar are inserted; the rest of the paper is peeled off, and string holding china marker is attached.

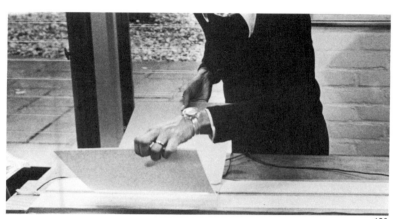

106

107

108

109 Before cutting one of the ends to size, an interior circular hole will be cut into it. To prepare for cutting hole, a space large enough for the saw blade to fit is drilled.

110 The blade is inserted, and sawing begins. The saw finds its way to the line indicating the hole, where it follows the line until the circle drops out.

Time Capsule

This calender is placed inside tubular material. For this design a calendar with one month per page should be purchased. The calendar pictured is made with 3-inch diameter (outside dimension) tubing. Tubing may be purchased in many other sizes.

1. Cut tubing to fit calendar. After trimming the borders of the purchased calendar, the width of the calendar used here is 11 inches.

2. The ends are made of ¼-inch clear material measuring 4½ inches square. One of the ends will have a 2½-inch hole cut out of it in order that there be an opening into which the calendar will be inserted and removed. When cutting a hole with the sabre saw, which is what I did here, it is easier to cut the hole in a large piece of material and then cut it to the square size. To cut an interior hole, first drill a hole into the center of the drawn circle. The hole should be large enough to accommodate the saw blade, as that is where the blade will enter the material. After the hole is made, insert the blade and then cut toward the line of the circle, and proceed to cut along the pencilled line. As the year progresses, pages will be removed as needed.

109

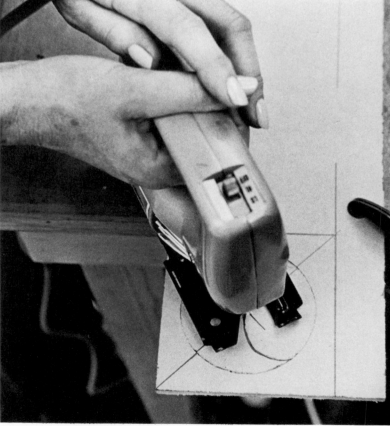

110

111 After the two ends have been cut, polished, and the masking tape removed, they are cemented to the ends of the tube.

112 One of the ends is a solid square, and the other is the one into which the hole was cut. It is into the latter that all of the pages of the calendar are inserted.

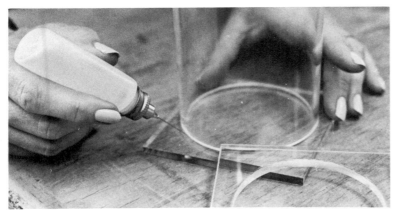

111

112

9. Designs on Demand

Ideas for designs come from unexpected sources: a passing word from someone who says, "Why don't they make . . .?" is usually the beginning of a new project. One day when I was visiting with Isabel O'Neil, she mentioned that she would like to have a good book "prop" for reading in bed. Remembering similar wishes all of those times when I stacked small pillows on my abdomen while trying to keep a book at the proper angle for bed reading, I decided to make the "O'Neil reader."

The O'Neil reader is made of $\frac{3}{16}$-inch opaque Plexiglas, is cut in one piece, and uses the strip heater for its fabrication. However, in order to figure out the design and the proper angles for the bends, I first cut it out from a material purchased at an art supply store. The material is called "foam core" and consists of a sheet of foam laminated between two pieces of white paper. After experimenting with the foam core, cutting it with an X-acto knife, and scoring it where I thought the bends should be, I decided upon the design.

The measurements are as follows: The over-all measurements of the cut piece are 18½ inches by 28¾ inches. There is a "C" curve cut out of one end 3½ inches from each side. The deepest point of the curve is 2½ inches. Two ⅜-inch holes should be drilled three inches apart, 13¾ inches from the end of the side where the C curve is cut. For the marks indicating where the bends will be, see illustration. A protractor is needed for measuring angles.

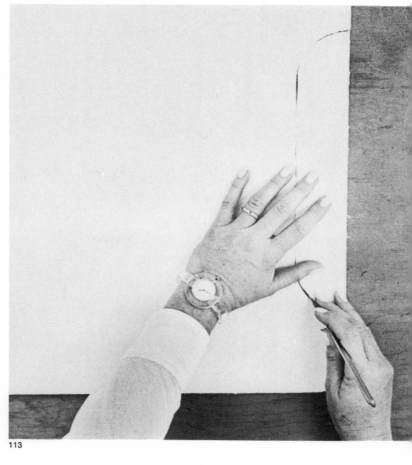

113

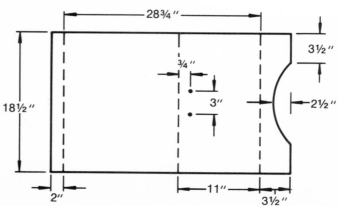

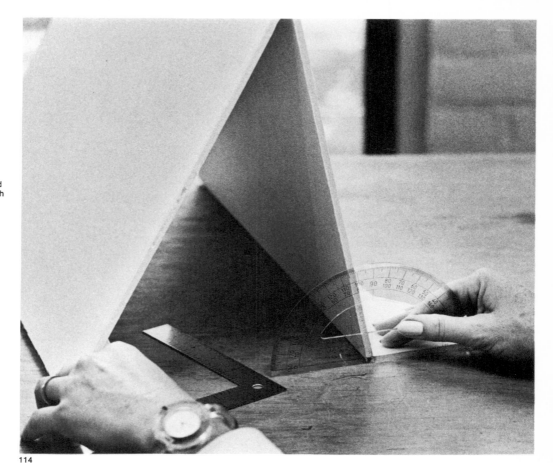

114 After angles are decided upon, they are measured with a protractor. The adjustable nature of the model permits many choices.

114

115 The material is cut using the sabre saw.

115

116 Masking paper had been peeled off prior to bending, but in order to protect the material while drilling, small pieces of masking tape have been applied.

117 The material has been placed on the strip heater using guide lines made with a china marker to help properly place the Plexiglas over the heating element.

118 But before heating actually takes place, those marks must be removed. Isopropyl alcohol and then water will remove the marks.

116

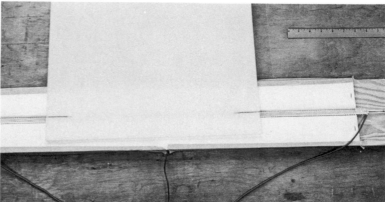

117

When using the strip heater to soften the material in order to make the bends, make the bend which will be at the bottom of the back (uncurved) end first. That first bend should have a 60-degree angle. The purpose for this bend is merely to prevent the edge of the material from cutting into your legs when the reader is in use.

The next bend is to form the top of the reader. This bend is heated on the same side of the material that the first one was. After sufficiently heating the material, make that bend to form a 50-degree angle. This will make the distance from front to back 9¼ inches.

The last bend is to form the shelf where the book will rest. This bend goes in the opposite direction from the other two. Therefore, the heating will be on the reverse side of the material, since the heated side is the outside of the bend. After this is heated, make the bend so that you achieve an 85-degree angle.

The purpose for the holes previously drilled is to attach cord with weights on the ends. This will hold the pages of the book back while the reader is in use. For this I used vinyl cord and attached slices of acrylic tubing.

118

Mrs. O'Neil liked the stand that I made for her, but we both thought it a little too heavy for comfort. Since I did not think that anything thinner than the ³⁄₁₆-inch material that had been used would be strong enough, I decided to cut a hole in the back of the stand. In order to do this, I had to re-protect the Plexiglas with masking tape, and cut an interior hole using first the drill and then the sabre saw, following the same method described in the section regarding making the calendar in the tube. The hole cut measured 9 inches in diameter. It did the trick! Now the reader was strong but light enough for comfortable use.

119

119 Making the first bend.

120 Reader in use. The vinyl cord with weights holds the pages back.

10. Make a Circle

The circle used aesthetically in the mobile can also be used in a number of ways for functional purposes. Its versatility is endless.

The first step in preparing to cut the circle is to cut a square from the sheet acrylic a little larger than you want the finished circle to be. After tracing the circle on the protective paper, cut the four corners from the square. Save the corners because, remember, they may be inspiration for a future work. With the sabre saw, cut your circle. It is advisable to use wood clamps to hold the material, moving them as necessary, in order for you to have two free hands to guide the saw. After scraping and sanding you are ready to polish your circle to a fine gleam. (If you do not have a saw, your plastics supplier will cut a circle for you.)

To give you an example of the versatility of the circle, let's start with circles of 9-inch diameter cut from sheet acrylic ¾₆ inches thick. What do they give you? Alone, they make place mats for the table, just the right size to fit under a plate. With half-balls cemented underneath, they make trivets for keeping hot food containers from harming the table. Bent in two places, they are holders for paper hand towels. Two of them will make a letter rack, with something left over!

121 The nine-inch diameter circle is cut and edge-finished.

122 Three half-balls cemented to the underside make it into a trivet for protecting table tops from hot serving dishes.

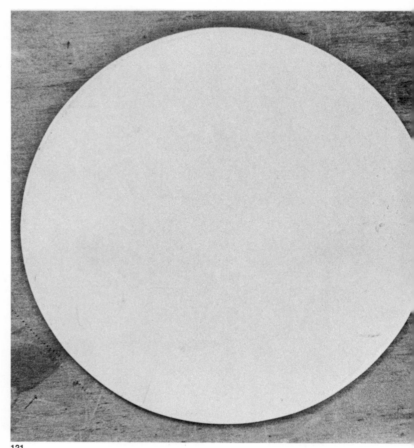

121

122

123 Using the method described in "Variations on a Theme," a path of masking paper is removed from the material where heating takes place.

124 The heating for the bending will be done twice, as there are two bends to be made.

125 Clamping the softened material against a right-angle aid while it is cooling insures a proper bend.

126 Folded towels fit perfectly in a pristine cradle of white Plexiglas.

123

124

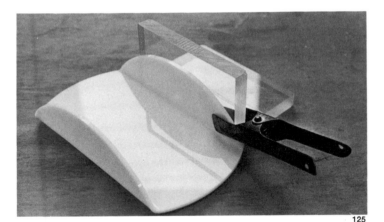

125

126

Paper Towel Holder

1. Do not remove the protective paper from the Plexiglas except in two 2-inch strips along the lines to be bent (see notes on p. 26). Find these lines by finding the diameter of the circle, and then measuring off a section that will be 4¾ inches. This will be the bottom of the holder. Paper towels are 4½ × 8½ inches when folded.

2. Be sure to have a guide handy that will keep your bends at right angles while cooling after they have been strip-heated. Heat the strip heater and prepare your piece by marking lightly with a china marker where the bends will be. These marks should be wiped off as soon as you have placed the Plexiglas directly over the center of the heating element before heating starts taking place.

3. Heating will take about seven minutes before material is soft enough to bend. Bend with heated side out, and clamp against your guide until cool. You are now ready to make the second bend in the same manner.

4. After peeling paper from the material, you can, if desired, put your half-balls as bumpers under the bottom of your holder. It is not necessary to do so, but it will make a more finished design.

127 After the first circle has been bent according to specifications, the second circle is divided into three equal parts.

128 The two inside pieces, are cemented into place,

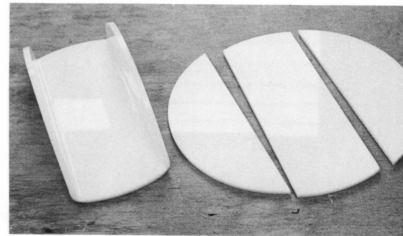

127

Letter Rack

An antique toast rack is the inspiration for a letter rack which can be made from two 9-inch circles.

1. Proceed as above to prepare for bending, this time making the bottom section 3 inches wide. However, because you will be cementing the two center sections, remove the protective paper on one side of the circle completely, and on the other side just remove it in strips from where the heating will take place.

2. Proceed to heat and bend on marked lines 3 inches apart on circle #1, using method described for making towel holder.

3. On circle #2 measure off three equal sections and cut. Put aside the center section; this will not be used. You will have, however, two dividers for the letter rack. Scrape and sand, but do not polish the cut edge. After dusting, place these two pieces 1 inch apart, equidistant from the center on circle #1. Cement in place.

4. Peel off the rest of the protective paper.

This is only the beginning. Numerous other things can be made from the circle. A hanging shelf can be made by making one bend and drilling a hole for hanging. A tray can be made by cementing tubular material on to form the gallery. A holder for stamps, pencils, etc., can be made in the same manner. Look around; you will find many inspirations to guide you.

128

129 and the letter rack is complete. (Stationery courtesy of Private Papers.)

130 Nothing is wasted. The surplus piece is bent to form a holder for a pad of note paper.

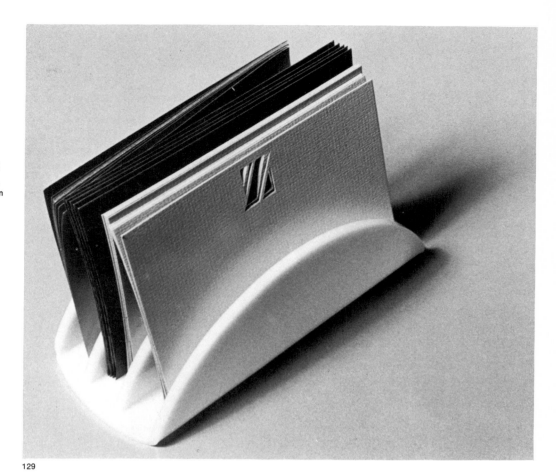

129

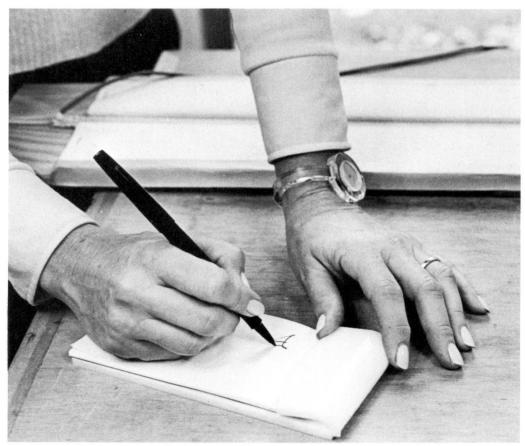

130

131 Disks may be made of
Plexiglas with engraved
mottos or decorated with
stones and findings.

132 It's a comfortable
adornment.

11. Make a Necklace, Candy Dish, and Serving Dish

To familiarize you with the technique of
heat forming, the first project we will make
is a bangle-type necklace. The necklace will
be made of the same cast rod you have
used for your practice sessions. The rod will
be cut 15 inches long and can be easily cut
with a hand-saw if necessary. Two half-balls
will also be needed. They should be ¼ inch
in diameter. They will be cemented to the
ends of the necklace.

131

133 The rod is cut with a handsaw while being held securely in vise.

134 Before the rod is formed into the necklace, the ends are sanded smooth.

135 To acquaint yourself with the heating process, a practice piece of rod is put into the oven.

136 To test its flexibility, it is tied into a knot.

137 After the necklace is ready for forming . . .

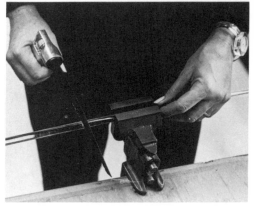

133

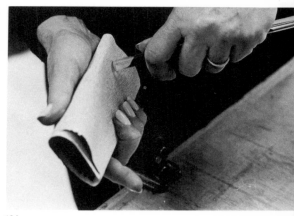

134

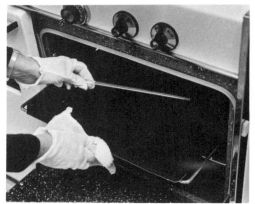

135

136

137

Before starting this project, it will be necessary to plan a jig (guide) on which to place your work while it is cooling. The one photographed is made of plywood. It consists of a depressed ¼-inch ring cut out of the wood in the shape of the finished necklace. It was made for me by a local carpenter.

1. After sanding the ends of the rod, pre-heat oven to 300° F., and place rod inside on Teflon-coated sheet. It would be helpful also to place in oven the knot you made during your practice sessions. Observing the change taking place in the knot as the heat makes it change its shape will help you to know when your material attains flexibility. Be sure that you are wearing your cotton gloves when touching the heated material. It will probably take about six minutes until it is ready for forming. At that point it is interesting to note that the knot has opened and through "memory" regained its original (flat) shape.

138 A

138 A and B it is put into the jig and covered in order that it remain flat.

139 When it has cooled, a half-ball is cemented to each end. To aid in holding these tiny half-balls, a piece of masking tape is used.

140 The necklace.

138 B

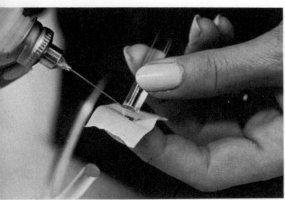

139

140

2. Quickly remove the rod from the oven, and place it into the jig. Cover the jig with flat board to insure that the material will lie flat. It will take but a few minutes to cool. Remove from the jig.

3. Cement half-balls to ends of necklace. As these are very tiny, enlist the aid of masking tape to help hold them in place for cementing.

Note that the necklace does not meet in the back. It is held in place on the neck by tension.

The medallion pictured is a round which I had cut and polished to order. It was hand engraved by a talented and accommodating man whom I found through the Yellow Pages. Perhaps you might try lettering yours with an electric engraver or maybe decorate a medallion with stones and acrylic polyester resin findings. If you cement the latter two, you will have to use the thicker, polymerized cement for this purpose as mentioned in the chapter on bonding.

141

Making a Candy Dish

While trying to think of projects to make to illustrate the technique of oven heating for

forming Plexiglas, I decided to use two circles, each 8 inches in diameter. The first circle, made of ¼-inch smoke color, was used to form a candy dish.

A mold for forming was improvised by using two Pyrex bowls of identical size, between which the softened material was placed. To help keep the tension required while my candy dish was cooling, I used two heavy weights. And to hurry the cooling process, the whole thing was immersed in water. For the ¼-inch material to reach forming stage, it was in the oven for ten minutes at 300° F.

142

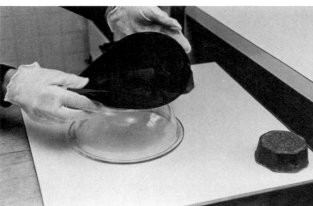

143

141 Candy Dish.

142 Softened material being taken from the oven. Gloves are worn to protect hands from the hot Plexiglas.

143 Softened material being placed on bowl from which it will take form.

144 A second bowl of the same size covers the softened material. Weights and pressure are exerted.

145 It is quickly put into water to cool.

144

145

Drape Forming to Make a Serving Dish

Softened material may be formed into a soft curve by hanging it over a form. In this case the weight of the material itself causes the form to shape. To illustrate this technique, I have made a serving dish out of the other circle. This one was ⅛ inch in thickness, and it took but four minutes to reach forming stage. For this project I also made use of kitchen utensils for helping to achieve the form required. This time I used a rolling pin. The serving dish looks just right for holding celery and olives.

146 Two bowls and a rolling pin are put into use as a form for drape forming.

147 The softened piece having just been taken from the oven is draped over the rolling pin.

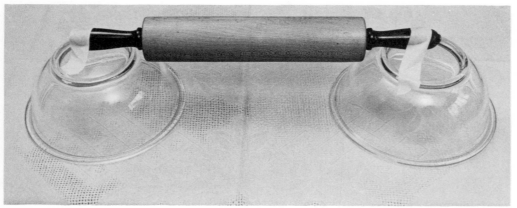

146

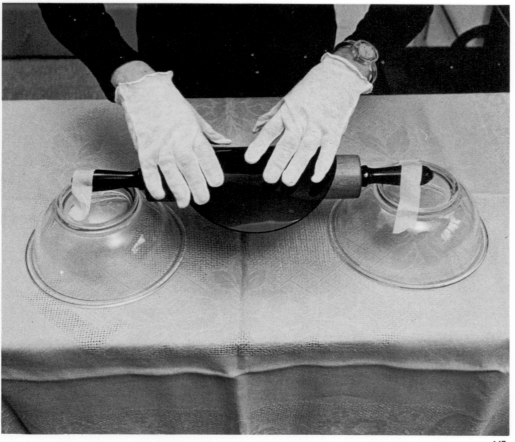

147

148 It is quickly dropped into water to cool.

149 Serving piece for Celery and Olives.

148

149

PART 3. PLEXIGLAS USED WITH OTHER MEDIA

12. Coffee Table with Terrarium

The current awareness of ecology combined with my ambition to design a piece of furniture for this book resulted in this Plexiglas coffee table with inserted terrarium.

The table, which measures 48 × 22 inches and is 17 inches high, uses 26 square feet of ¼-inch Plexiglas. The two domes which form the terrarium are made of blown thermo-formed sheet acrylic. The domes may be purchased in various sizes at stores that carry plastic materials or through mail order, where they may be made to your specific size requirements (see Sources of Supply for information). The domes should have a 1-inch flange, and after purchase the edges should be polished to a high gloss.

1. Cut, or have cut, a rectangle for the table top measuring 48 × 22 inches. On one end of the top, a hole will get cut into which the terrarium will fit. On the protective masking paper, pencil the outline for the hole. With the aid of a compass or other guide, draw a circle 18 inches in diameter, allowing 3 inches at the end of the table and 2 inches on each side as a margin around the dome. Cut the hole according to the technique shown in the instructions for making the time capsule, Chapter 8.

2. The legs and apron are cut from two 21½ × 16¾-inch rectangles and two that measure 48 × 16¾ inches. Before cutting, mark with pencil on the protective masking paper. In order to avoid having sharp angles where the legs and aprons meet, drill a ¼-inch hole at the point of contact 2⅞ inches from the top edge and 2⅝ inches from each vertical edge, and then proceed to cut toward the holes from each direction. This will give a slightly rounded angle at the inside corner of each leg.

3. In order to prevent the terrarium from shifting, four holes of ⅜-inch diameter are drilled into the flanges of the dome which correspond with holes in a spacer, which will be described later in these instructions. Into these holes, a flat-headed aluminum rivet ¾ inch long will be inserted.

4. After all of the pieces have been cut and edge-finished to a fine gleam, the table is cemented together with thin solvent.

5. While humidity is a requirement for growing plants in a terrarium, excess moisture will cause fogging; therefore a small amount of air should be permitted to enter. To allow for this you may cement four small (¼-inch diameter) half-balls on the underside of the top dome. Or, using two pieces of scrap material, you may cut two dividers, curved to fit, which have holes aligned with those drilled into the domes. These may be used when necessary to allow air to enter the terrarium and may be removed if desired (see illustration).

You will find that after cutting out the legs and apron, you are left with two small rectangles and two large. So as not to waste this material, you could make either a six-sided cube by cutting the larger rectangles in half horizontally, or a pedestal, if the larger rectangles are cut in half vertically.

150 The modern lines of the table are pleasing in combination with a traditional setting.

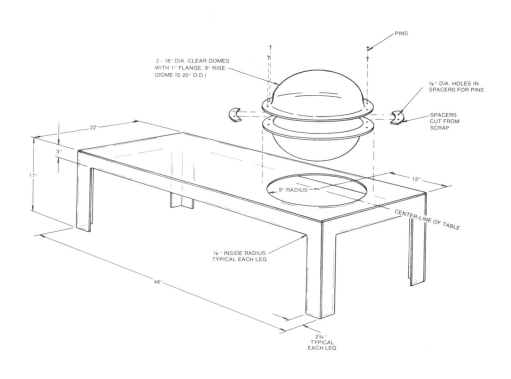

2 - 18" DIA. CLEAR DOMES
WITH 1" FLANGE, 9" RISE.
(DOME IS 20" O.D.)

PINS

⅛" DIA. HOLES IN
SPACERS FOR PINS

SPACERS
CUT FROM
SCRAP

22"

3"

17"

9" RADIUS

12"

CENTER-LINE OF TABLE

⅛" INSIDE RADIUS
TYPICAL EACH LEG

48"

2¾"
TYPICAL
EACH LEG

150

13. Showcases to Present and Preserve

The Yam mask, a ceremonial artifact from New Guinea, presents an interesting juxtaposition between the old and the new. To enhance the polychrome-decorated wood carving, a severe, elongated pedestal is made of a solid block of clear Plexiglas. The mechanics employed to hold the mask on the base include a ¼-inch-square rod made of clear material. This is attached by cementing into a groove that has been cut out of the block. To hold the mask to the rod, I have tied a piece of monofilament around a scored notch in the rod. The monofilament is virtually invisible and does not intrude.

The bronze head, memento of a trip to the Far East, merely needs a square of clear material into which a peg is cemented.

151

152

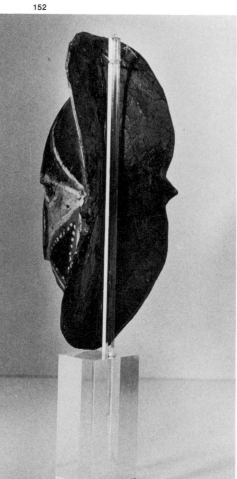

153

154 *The Show-off* for displaying jewelry between wearings.

155 Pin cushion with needlepoint.

156 Needlepoint sandwiched between two sections of a tray produces an interesting design.

154

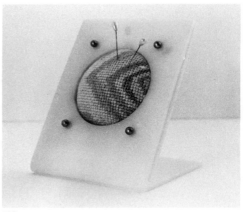

155

Semi-precious jewelry may be taken out of the bureau drawer to be used as an art object when not being worn. It may be displayed on the "show-off." This is an easel which has been bent with the aid of the strip heater. Its ¼-inch thickness gives the illusion of being much thicker because the edges have been beveled prior to polishing. A slice of clear tubing has been cemented on the easel to form a frame for the little treasure.

The great rage for needlework led me to design the tray which does double duty. It may be used as a tray and also as another means of using needlepoint. The pin cushion on its Plexiglas easel was a natural follow-up of the tray.

156

157

It would be presumptuous to think that one could improve upon art such as the two small sculptures by Arp pictured here. But you can see that another dimension has been added by the design of the stands upon which these have been placed. Formerly the pieces were destined to hang flatly on a wall.

Solid rod of varying lengths, a hollow cube, and some small half-balls give an underwater illusion to the smoke-colored, transparent acrylic shadow box used for displaying shells. The front is clear acrylic.

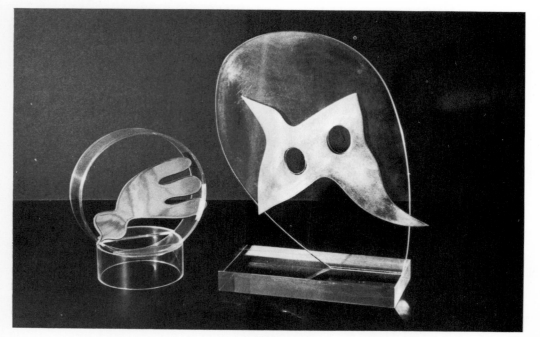

157 *The Shell Collection.*

158 Two Plexiglas stands for displaying the work of Jean Arp.

158

159 *Light Box* (Collection of
Mr. and Mrs. James Grad,
Lake Success, New York.
Photograph by Eric Pollitzer).

160 *New York Is a House of
Cards* (Collection of Mr. and
Mrs. Noel Levine. New York
Photograph by Eric Pollitzer).

159

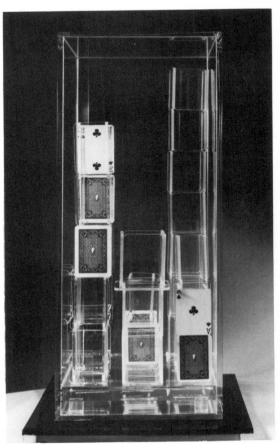

160

14. Games We Play

It was a game that began my commercial career. It seemed so natural to combine the aesthetic qualities of a jigsaw puzzle made of Plexiglas with the challenge that solving it provoked. And that is the way Pencentrics was born! The combination of an art object, looking good just sitting on a table top with its lines and spaces making an ever-changing design, or partially put together with some of its components looking like a pile of ice cubes, also being a challenging puzzle keeping its audience busy for literally hours of intense concentration are the qualities that made Pencentrics a success.

Jigsaw Puzzle

To make your own version you will need a square of ½-inch clear material measuring 8 × 8 inches. Finish the edges to a satin, not polished, finish.

With the aid of a ruler, draw the design on the protective paper. I suggest that you follow my formula of using many pieces that at first glance seem to be the same size and shape. This makes the solution more challenging than if there were to be obvious differences. Cut the parts on designated lines and scrape and sand with 200 no-load silicone carbide paper. The reason for not polishing the edges to a high gloss is because the design when the puzzle is assembled is more apparent if the edges are opaque in combination with the shiny surface of the acrylic material.

The frame for holding the puzzle is made of transparent smoke color, Plexiglas #2412 bronze, ¼ inch thick.

Cut the bottom piece ¹⁄₁₆ inch larger than the puzzle. This will facilitate removing and assembling when the puzzle is being solved. The sides will need two strips 8³⁄₁₆ × ½ inch and two strips 8¹⁄₁₆ × ½ inch. After polishing the edges, cement to the *outside* of the base. This will give you a wall going ¼ inch above the base to encase the puzzle. As the puzzle is ½ inch thick, part of it will be above the frame when assembled. Add small half-balls under each corner. This will raise the frame to let light pass underneath, adding the properties of light refraction and reflection to the design.

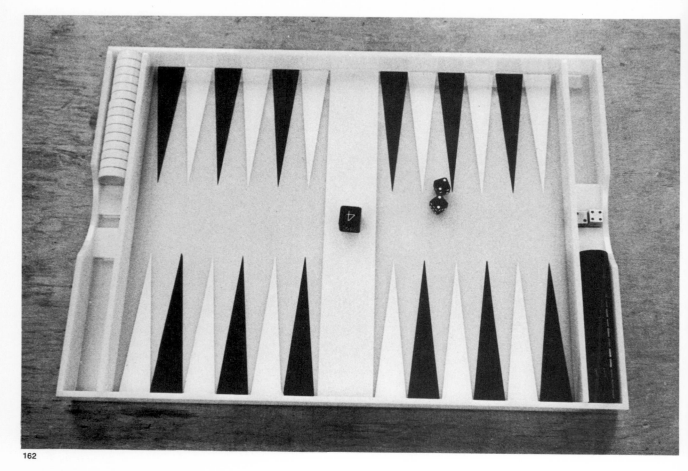

162

Backgammon Board

The classic game of backgammon is another decorative, geometric design used as the pattern for a table game.

For the backgammon set shown here, a combination of Plexiglas and Krylon spray paint is used. Our version will have a double function, as it will combine a tray, usable just as such, with a removable insert containing the pattern for the playing board.

The tray pictured is made of yellow opaque Plexiglas in ¼-inch stock. You will need a piece for the bottom measuring 25 × 18 inches, and four pieces for the sides. Two of the side pieces will measure 25 × 1½ inches, and two 17½ × 1½ inches. The two shorter sides should have a C curve cut out for ease in carrying. This should measure 4¾ × ¾ inches over-all. Polish edges, and cement the sides on top of base. Add four ½-inch half-balls to each corner of under side of tray.

For the insert containing the playing board you will need a sheet of clear material ⅛ inch thick measuring 24½ × 17½ inches. You will also need a strip of yellow material measuring 2½ × 17½ inches. This will be a divider for the board.

163

164

162 The board, ready for play.

163 The tray is made by first cementing together the four pieces that form the frame.

164 Completed tray used for serving.

165 Using a metal ruler, kerosene, and the special paper removal tool, the points are scored on previously pencil-marked lines.

166 Alternate points are removed.

167 The first color is spray painted on. The dark color first.

168 Now the remaining points are removed . . .

169 and the second color is applied.

165

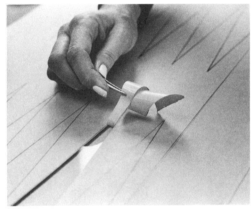

166

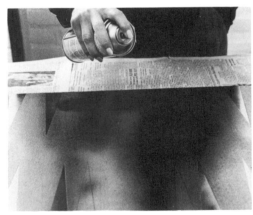

167

Two strips of yellow 1⅜ × 17½ inches, and four squares 1½ × 1½ inches will complete the material for the board, along with two colors of Krylon spray paint. In the board pictured, white and green were used. The Fletcher-Terry masking paper stripping tool described on page 13 will be used. Be sure to have either kerosene or mineral spirits for use with that tool. Those unfamiliar with the stripping tool might be more comfortable using an X-acto knife instead. In either case, kerosene or mineral spirits should be used to help in the removal of the adhesive holding the masking paper to the surface of the Plexiglas.

After edge finishing the clear sheet, draw the pattern for the board on the protective paper. A border of 1¾ inches should be left on both ends of the long side of the rectangle. This will be where the compartments for the tiles and dice will be placed. There will also be a space 2½ inches wide left in the center. The pattern will consist of four sections of design, each nine inches long. The design consists of six elongated triangles 1⅜ inches wide and seven inches long. I suggest that you employ the aid of graph paper to help plan your design.

Before starting to work, please note that the painting will be done on the reverse side of the clear Plexiglas, as constant use would wear the paint.

Using the stripping tool or X-acto knife, and following the instructions given on page 26, remove the paper from every other triangle and spray with the green paint. Be sure that the paper left on the board is adhering in order that you may get a clean edge with your paint. If necessary, add a bit of masking tape. After this is dry, repeat on the alternate triangles with the white paint. Consult the directions on the spray can as to the length of time between coats. As this is being done on the reverse side of the material, it is important to spray with the dark color first, as the second spraying will cover not only the unpainted triangles, but the ones previously sprayed as well, and there might otherwise be a chance that the dark color might show through the white. After the paint has dried, peel the paper from the rest of the board.

168

169

170 After all of the remaining paper has been removed from the sheet, the opaque strips are placed and cemented on reverse side.

171 This gives you two units, the tray and a removable playing board.

Turn the painted sheet over, and on the unpainted side, after edge finishing the pieces of yellow mentioned above, place the 2½-inch wide strip flat side down on the center of the board, thus dividing the board in two, and cement. The remaining pieces will be cemented standing on edge. The strips 17½ × 1⅜ inches should be placed 1½ inches from each end of the board, and the four 1½-inch squares placed flat seven inches from each end, forming compartments measuring 7 × 1½ inches. The compartments in the middle thus formed will store the dice.

Tiles for playing are 1½-inch circles made of opaque ½-inch material. They often may be purchased ready-made where plastic materials are sold.

170

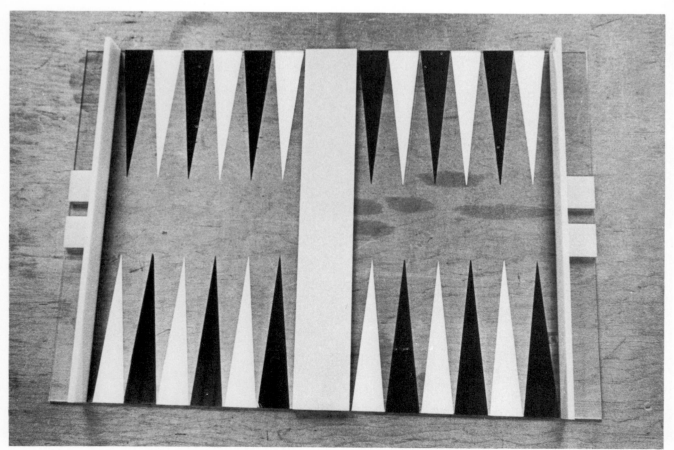

171

PART 4. MAKE A MONUMENT

172 The Monument.

172

The triangles used in *Mobile #1* have inspired many other constructions. Among them is this large-scale sculpture that I planned for display out of doors, where its facets act as prisms, catching sunlight and reflecting the colors of nature.

The model for this piece is made of the left-over triangles just as they were when I was given them. They were not edge finished; their only function was to be used as a small, preliminary design for the monumental piece. The model is cemented together, and it was not until I planned the material for the final piece to be 1 inch thick that I realized that another method for attaching the triangular pieces would have to be used. I could not risk air bubbles trapped in the seams, spoiling the beauty of the design.

173

174 Marking the triangles with numbers will help the assembling.

175 In order to see how it will look enlarged, a model is made of Foam-core held together with masking tape.

173 The maquette, as small as a match box.

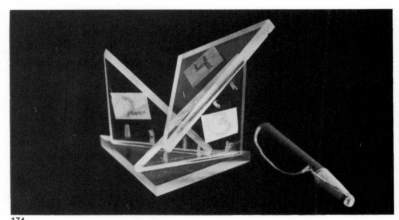

174

175

Before deciding on the size, and in order to see how the final piece would look enlarged, I cut four triangles out of Foam-core (the foam and paper laminate found in art supply stores) in various degrees of enlargement until I decided to make the relative scale 1 inch to 1 foot. The final sculpture is made of two 2-foot squares cut diagonally to form four triangles of equal size. The method of fabrication decided upon uses hardened steel dowel pins set into holes drilled to hold them. Steel dowel pins may be purchased in a hardware supply store that specializes in parts for machines. The placement of the dowel pins was planned not only to give the piece stability but also to divide the spaces artistically. The dowel pins thus become part of the design.

The finished piece is most successful. I can see it now further enlarged. How grand it would look 8 feet tall!

176

176 A rubber mallet is used
to hammer the rivets in place.

177 The last piece is fitted
into place.

177

178 Mrs. Zahn decides to put it in the garden.

179 The Monument photographed indoors on a base made of mirrored
Plexiglas. The shape of the base echoes the triangular shape of the
construction. The mirror on the top of the base reflects the glittering image
of the construction, accented by the reflections of the steel dowels. The
sides reflect the wooden floor, making the piece seem to float in space.

178

179

PART 5. YES, BUT WILL IT SELL?

The success that you have in making some of the articles described in this book and the experience of cutting your own designs will probably lead to the question: "What will happen if I try to market my design, will it sell?" Yes, it will sell, and you will be well received by merchants, who are always on the alert for new products that excite the imagination.

Before trying to sell your product, a sample will have to be made, and you will have to know just how to go about having it produced in the quantity needed. If the design is simple, you might be able to start producing it yourself. The successful designer of the much-copied (but now protected by patent) cook-book holder told me that she started to produce that item at home, engaging the help of all her family. It was after a hot summer over the strip-heater that orders became so numerous that she was forced to find a fabricator to manufacture for her.

Fabricators are listed in the Yellow Pages under "Plastics, fabricating, finishing and decorating." There are fabricators who execute one-of-a-kind items; in fact, it is a fabricator in this category who produces the costly editions for a famous sculptor who works in Plexiglas. There are also fabricators who will copy in quantity your studio-made sample. It is the latter whom you will want to fill your orders.

Try it. You might find yourself with a success on your hands. And you certainly will find yourself excitingly busy and stimulated.

With me, it all started with the puzzle "Pencentrics," and progressed through a succession of other designs for a rewarding few years, culminating with this book. Perhaps it would be helpful for me to tell you of my first experiences with manufacturing when I designed "Pencentrics."

After designing the first sample of the puzzle, I called upon a store in New York, well known for its contemporary, well-designed merchandise. I showed three patterns for the design to the buyer and merchandise man, and after they selected the one that they liked best, we talked about some details regarding marketing this product. They pointed out to me that the puzzle had to

have a diagram to package with it. I knew approximately how the puzzle would have to be priced in order for it to sell, and despite my knowing that the amount of heavy (½ inch thick) material used in its manufacture would make it costly to produce, I was determined for it to sell at a realistic price.

After another visit with the same two gentlemen, I was given an order for three dozen puzzles. My next step was to find someone to produce my product. I was fortunate in being guided to a fine fabricator. The price for making puzzles had to be based on a large quantity to be made at one time in order for the ultimate retail cost to be as I had planned. You can understand that it is more practical for a fabricator to cut his material and set up for production a larger amount of merchandise rather than several smaller amounts of the same merchandise. I therefore asked for a price based on ordering a hundred puzzles at a time.

Having sold only 36, I was faced with the necessity of disposing of the other 64 before I placed my order. I was lucky. The puzzle had a lot of appeal, and my timing was right. My first order turned out to be 200 rather than 100! My education was not yet completed, as I then had to find the boxes in which to pack my puzzles. Lack of experience made this a rather costly proposition, as the boxes had to be made to a specific size for an exact fit. Thinking it over since, I have decided that if I were to do it all over again, I would find out in what sizes stock boxes are made, and make the puzzle fit the box!

"Pencentrics" was very successful and many hundreds were sold. The puzzle launched my own present career, and every new project brought new challenges and new solutions. And without knowing that it was happening, I became educated in selling, producing, shipping, and even bookkeeping. The design for the puzzle has never ceased to please me. I use its pattern as a logo on my stationery and calling cards, and had a copy made in silver to wear as a memento of this first, happy experience with the world of business.

180

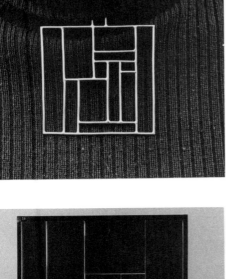

181

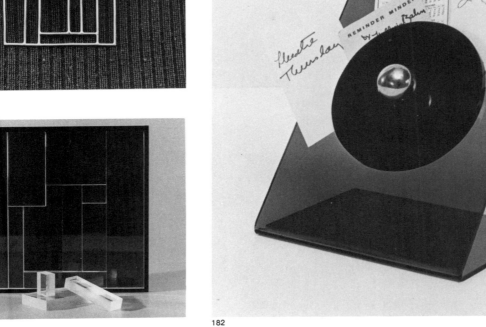

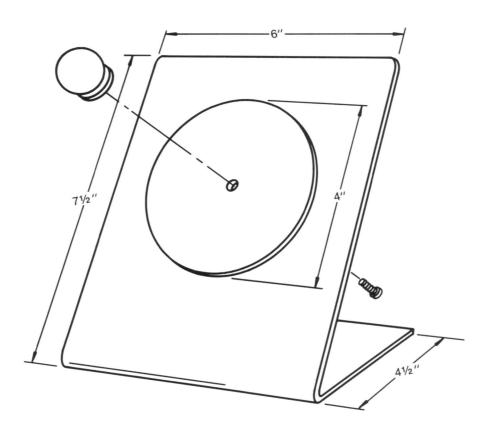

182

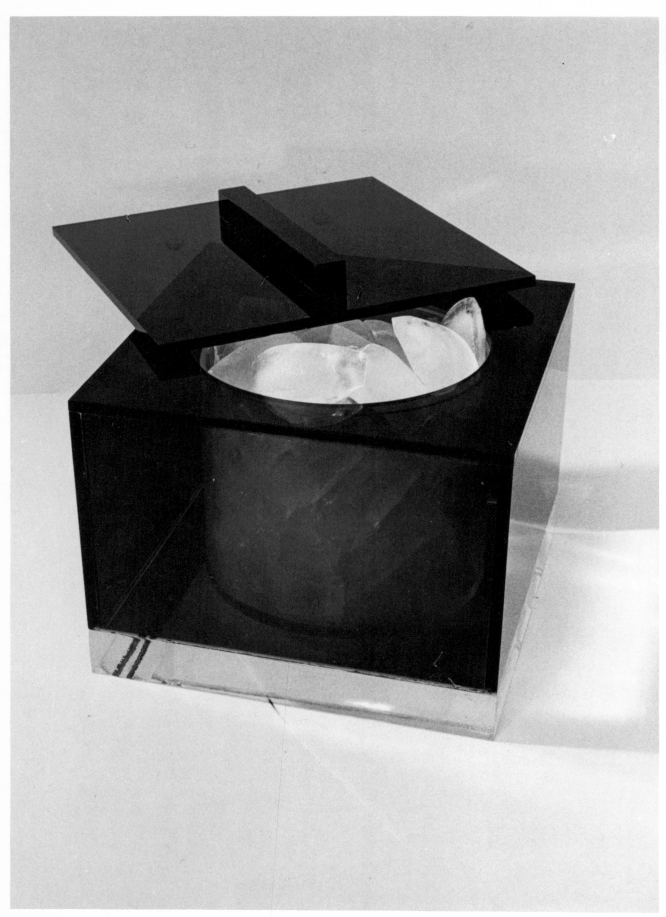

183

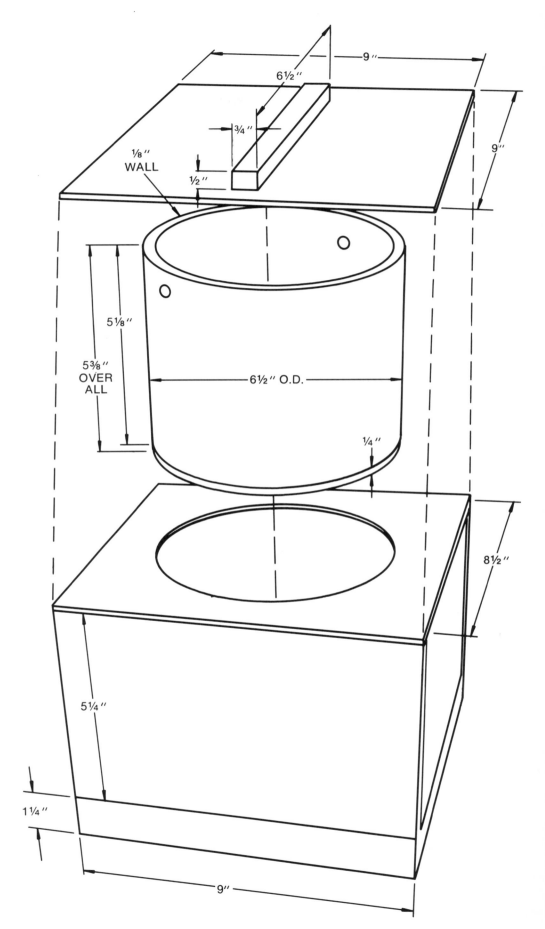

9 "

6½ "

¾ "

⅛ "
WALL

½ "

9 "

5⅛ "

5⅜ "
OVER
ALL

6½ " O.D.

¼ "

8½ "

5¼ "

1¼ "

9"

183 Ice bucket made of ¼-
inch transparent smoke
(bronze) material with 1¼-
inch clear bottom. The
removable liner is made of
⅛-inch wall tubular material
6½ inches in diameter
(outside dimensions). Two
half-balls attached to the
inside of the liner aid in the
removal of the liner and four
half-balls on the underside of
the lid keep it from sliding
out of place. The bar on the
lid is made of opaque black
½-inch material.

184

184 Picture frames.

185 Show-off.

185

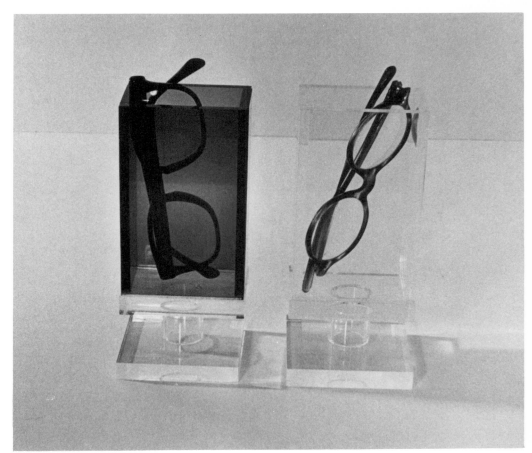

186 Eyeglass stands.

187 Lap trays.

186

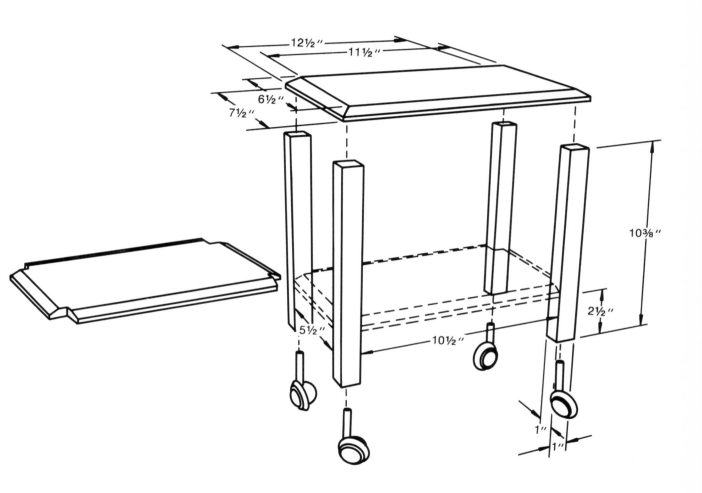

188 Telephone table, top,
and shelf are made of ½-inch
opaque material, legs of
1-inch. The bevel on the
surfaces gives a look of
weight to the top and shelf.
"Shepheard" casters, 1½ inch
diameter, are inserted into
the legs.

189 Necessaire. This handy desk organizer is made of ⅛-inch clear material with cups of 3-inch (o.d.) tubes, ⅛ inch thick.

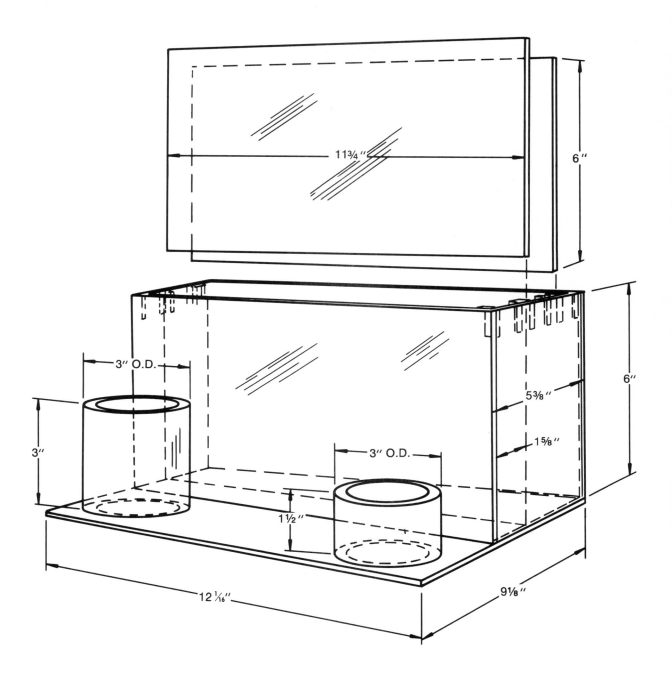

190 A & B. Two sizes of trays for inserting needlepoint design. The accompanying sketch has dimensions of the smaller tray. The trays are made of opaque material with a piece of clear material cemented to the form in order to protect the needlepoint.

190 A

190 B

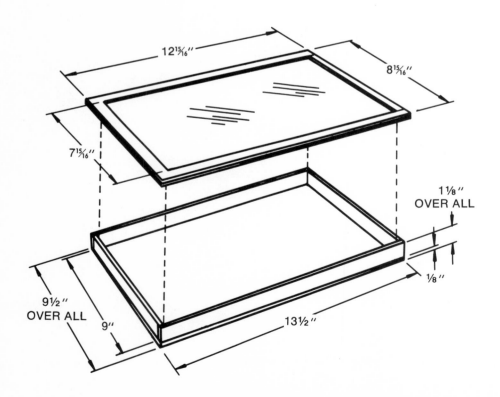

12¹⁵⁄₁₆″

8¹⁵⁄₁₆″

7¹⁵⁄₁₆″

1⅛″
OVER ALL

⅛″

9½″
OVER ALL

9″

13½″

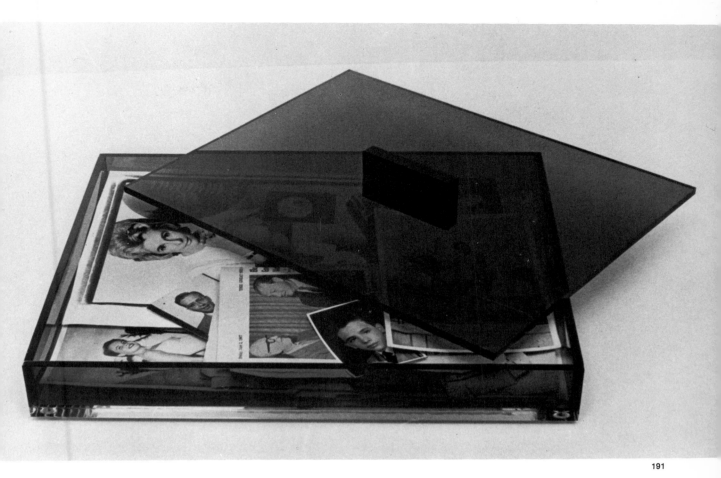

191

191 Photo tray made of ¼-
inch transparent smoke
(bronze) material with ½-inch
clear bottom. Bar on lid is
½-inch-thick opaque black.
Outside dimensions 12 x 15
inches.

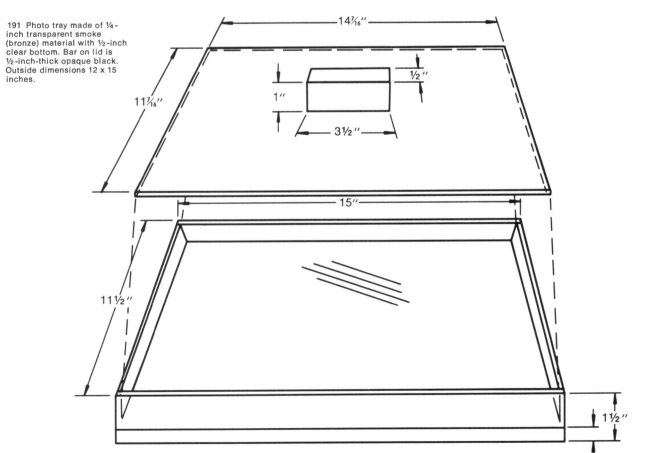

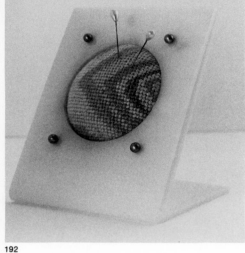

192

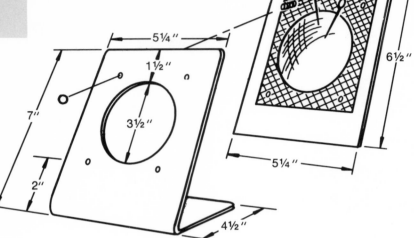

192 Pinpark. This is made of
³⁄₁₆-inch opaque material.
The canvas is held in place
by a solid piece behind the
cut-out front. The two sections
are attached by means of
brass balls held on ⅝-inch-
long screws.

193

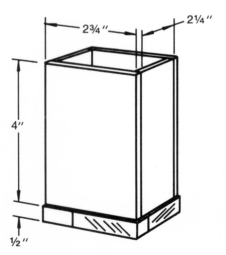

193 Planters and pencil cups
made of opaque material ¼
inch thick with clear ½-inch
bottoms.

If you decide to market any of your designs,
I hope that this chapter has been helpful
to you. I have just two words of advice: be
original. Your attempts can lead to a rich,
rewarding experience only if creativity is the
ingredient you combine with ambition.

Sources of Supply

Asterisks * indicate companies that sell by mail order as well as over the counter.

PLASTICS

ARIZONA

Phoenix
*Cadillac Plastic & Chemical
2625 University Dr., 85034

ARKANSAS

Little Rock
*Cope Plastics
2000 E. 17th St.

CALIFORNIA

Anaheim
*Cadillac Plastic & Chemical
1531 State Coll. Blvd., 92806

Berkeley
*Corth Plastics
725 Delaware St., 95071

Los Angeles Area
Plastic Center, Inc.
186 S. Alvarado St., 90057

Montebello
*Port Plastics, Inc.
8037 Slauson Ave., 90640

N. Hollywood
Gem-O-Lite
5525 Cahuenga Blvd., 91601

Sacramento
*Terrell's Plastics
3618 Broadway, 95817

San Diego
Ridout Plastics
1875 Hancock St., 92110

San Francisco Area
Menlo Park
*Port Plastics
180 Constitution Dr., 94025

Mountainview
Plastic Center, Inc.
1170 Terrabella Ave., 94040

Redwood City
*Corth Plastics
532 Howland St., 94063

COLORADO

Denver
*Plasticrafts
2800 N. Speer, 80211

Englewood
*Regal Plastic Supply Co.
3985 S. Kalamath, 80116

CONNECTICUT

Bridgeport
Modern Plastics
678 Howard Ave., 06605

E. Hartford
*Commercial Plastics
100 Prestige Park Rd., 06108

Orange
*Commercial Plastics
463 Boston Post Rd., 06477

CANADA

Montreal
*Commercial Plastics
5655 Blvd. de Maisonneuve W.

Ottawa
*Commercial Plastics
28 Capital Dr.

Toronto
*Commercial Plastics
300 Bridgeland Ave.

FLORIDA

Hialeah
Modern Plastics
7175 W. 20th Ave., 33014

Jacksonville
*Commercial Plastics
2331 Laura St., 32206

Miami
*Commercial Plastics
3801 N.W. Second Ave., 33127

Orlando
Modern Plastics
580 Fairville Rd., 32808
*Commercial Plastics
4096 S. Orange Ave., 32806

Pensacola
Modern Plastics
913 N. P St., 32505

St. Petersburg
Modern Plastics
2850 47th Ave. N., 33714

Tampa
*Faulkner Plastics
4504 E. Hillsborough Ave., 33601

West Palm Beach
Heyer Distributors
435 Southern Blvd., 33405

GEORGIA

Atlanta
*Commercial Plastics
334 North Ave. N.W., 30318

HAWAII

Honolulu
Hawaii Plastics
568 Dillingham Blvd., 96811

ILLINOIS

Franklin Park
Almac Plastics
10129 Pacific Ave., 60131

Godfrey
*Cope Plastics Inc.
1111 West Delmar Ave., 62035

IOWA

Des Moines
*Van Horn Plastics
8000 University Ave., 50311

Cedar Rapids
*Cope Plastics
714-66th Ave. S.W., 52404

KANSAS

Wichita
Regal Plastics
329 Indiana St., 67214
Star Lumber Co.
325 S. West St.

MARYLAND

Baltimore
*Almac Plastics of Maryland
6311 Erdman Ave., 21205

MASSACHUSETTS

Somerville
Commercial Plastics
352 McGrath Highway, 02143

MICHIGAN

Grand Rapids
*Almac Plastics of Michigan
2882 36th St. S.E., 49058

Warren
*Almac Plastics of Michigan
26004 Groesbeck Highway, 48090

MISSOURI

Kansas City
Regal Plastics Supply
2023 Holmes St., 64141

St. Louis
*Cope Plastics Missouri
6340 Knox Industrial Dr., 63139

NEBRASKA

Omaha
Regal Plastics
2324 Vinton St., 68108

NEW JERSEY

Newark
*Almac Plastics of New Jersey
171 Fabyan Pl., 07112

NEW MEXICO

Albuquerque
*Regal Plastics
3019 Princeton N.E., 87106

NEW YORK

Buffalo
Great Lakes Plastic
2371 Broadway, 14212

New York City Area

Ain Plastics
65 Fourth Ave., N.Y.C. 10003
*Almac Plastics
47-42 37th St., Long Island City 11101
Industrial Plastics
324 Canal St., N.Y.C. 10013

Farmingdale
Commercial Plastics and Supply Corp.
55 Main St., 11735

NORTH CAROLINA

Gibsonville
Engineered Plastics, Inc.
Box 108, 29249

Raleigh
*Commercial Plastics
731 W. Hargett St., 27611

OHIO

Akron
*Almac Plastics of Ohio
30 N. Summit St., 44308

Dayton
*Dayton Plastics
2554 Needmore Rd., 45414

OKLAHOMA

Oklahoma City
*Cope Plastics
105 N.E. 38th Terrace, 73105

Tulsa
*Plastic Engineering
6801 E. 44, 74145
*Ted's Hobbies Unlimited
11122 E. Admiral Place

OREGON

Portland
Universal Plastics
910 S.E. Star St., 97214

PENNSYLVANIA

Philadelphia
Almac Plastics of Pennsylvania
2031 Byberry Rd., 19116
Plastics of Philadelphia
Corner 12th and Arch Sts., 19107

Pittsburgh
*Commercial Plastics
2022 Chateau St., 15233

PUERTO RICO

San Juan
*Commercial Plastics
Avenida Fernandez Juncos 635, 00902

RHODE ISLAND

E. Providence
*Commercial Plastics
920 Broadway, 02974

SOUTH CAROLINA

Greenville
Engineered Plastics
Pleasantburg Industrial Park, 29607

TENNESSEE

Memphis
*Norrell, Inc.
721 Scott St., 38112

TEXAS

Dallas
*Commercial Plastics
2200 Vantage St., 75207

Houston
A-1 Plastics of Houston
5822 Southwest Freeway, 77027

VIRGINIA

Richmond
Engineered Plastics
5410 Distributor Dr., 23225
Plywood and Plastics
1727 Arlington Rd., 23230

WASHINGTON

Seattle
*Cadillac Plastic
2427 6th Ave. South, 98134
Universal Plastics
650 S. Industrial Way

DOMES FOR TERRARIUM

NEW JERSEY

Burlington
Stan Cook
*Cook's General Machine Shop
617 S. Lawrence St., P.O. Box 302, 08016

NEW YORK

Whitestone
*Plasti-vue Corp.
150-38 12th Ave., 11357

TOOLS AND CHEMICALS

Mail order only for tools, chemicals, etc.

Rohm and Haas
Tools for Plexiglas
P.O. Box 14619, Philadelphia, Pa., 19134

HARDWARE

NEW YORK

New York City Area
Simons Hardware
421 Third Ave., N.Y.C. 10016

Great Neck
Kolson Korenge
653 Middle Neck Rd., 11023